TREASURE-HOUSE OF MYSTERIES

Explorations of the Sacred Text
through Poetry in the Syriac Tradition

ST VLADIMIR'S SEMINARY PRESS
Popular Patristics Series
Number 45

The Popular Patristics Series published by St Vladimir's Seminary Press provides readable and accurate translations of a wide range of early Christian literature to a wide audience—students of Christian history to lay Christians reading for spiritual benefit. Recognized scholars in their fields provide short but comprehensive and clear introductions to the material. The texts include classics of Christian literature, thematic volumes, collections of homilies, letters on spiritual counsel, and poetical works from a variety of geographical contexts and historical backgrounds. The mission of the series is to mine the riches of the early Church and to make these treasures available to all.

Series Editor
BOGDAN BUCUR

Associate Editor
IGNATIUS GREEN

* * *

Series Editor
1999–2020
JOHN BEHR

Treasure-House of Mysteries

EXPLORATIONS OF THE SACRED TEXT THROUGH POETRY IN THE SYRIAC TRADITION

SEBASTIAN BROCK

ST VLADIMIR'S SEMINARY PRESS
YONKERS, NEW YORK

Library of Congress Cataloging-in-Publication Data

Treasure-house of mysteries : explorations of the sacred text through poetry in the Syriac tradition / [edited by] Sebastian Brock.
    p. cm. — (Popular patristics series, ISSN 1555–5755 ; no. 45)
    Includes bibliographical references and index.
    ISBN 978–0–88141–421–9
    1. Christian poetry, Syriac. I. Brock, Sebastian P.

PJ5617.T74 2012
892'.3—dc23

2011041767

ST VLADIMIR'S SEMINARY PRESS
575 Scarsdale Road, Yonkers, NY 10707
1-800-204-2665
www.svspress.com

ISBN 978–088141–421–9
ISSN 1555–5755

PRINTED IN THE UNITED STATES OF AMERICA

For Helen

and

for Susan and Alison

Contents

Introduction

All too often Christian tradition is thought of as having just two main strands, the "Greek East" (representing the various Orthodox Churches) and the "Latin West" (representing the Roman Catholic and Reformed Churches). This bipartite model totally ignores a third strand, which can for convenience be designated as the "Syriac Orient": whereas the Greek East and the Latin West represent essentially European traditions of Christianity, the Syriac Orient has its roots (as indeed does Christianity itself) in western Asia (the Middle East, seen from a European perspective).[1] This third strand is represented today by the various indigenous Middle Eastern churches, among which are several specifically of Syriac liturgical tradition (Syrian Orthodox, Syrian Catholic, Maronite, Church of the East, and Chaldean Catholic, together with their counterparts in South India). The connection with Syriac is significant, in that Syriac is a dialect of Aramaic, the Palestinian form of which was spoken by Jesus. This link is important for a number of reasons.

In the first place, Syriac became the literary language of Aramaic-speaking Christians all over the less hellenized parts of the Middle East at an early date. One consequence of this is the fact that the wording of the Lord's Prayer in Syriac, as it is still used in some of these Churches today, is almost identical with the Aramaic wording of Jesus' prayer, underlying the Greek Gospels, as reconstructed by scholars. More importantly, this link with Palestinian Aramaic also

---

[1]For the significance of this third strand of Christian tradition, see my "The Syriac Orient: a third 'lung' for the Church?," in *Orientalia Christiana Periodica* 71 (2005), pp. 5–20.

means that early Syriac literature, and especially its poetry, is far closer to the Jewish and biblical roots of Christianity than are early Christian texts in Greek or Latin. This is especially relevant when one comes to the understanding and interpretation of the biblical text, for it is here that one can find a wonderfully fresh and creative approach to the Bible, above all in the poetic texts.

Since Syriac literature is little known outside the small number of specialists, the main purpose of this collection of translations is to make available to a wider readership a selection of poems that deal specifically with biblical topics. Short introductions are provided for each poem, but annotation is kept to a minimum, for it seems much the best to let the poems speak for themselves; since, however, many of them are replete with biblical allusions that the modern reader may not always catch, references to the more important ones are indicated in the margins. A preliminary chapter outlines the approach to interpreting the biblical text that underlies all the authors of these poems; for this purpose I have concentrated on the many explicit comments on this subject to be found in the writings of the greatest of all Syriac poets, Ephrem.

Ephrem belongs to the fourth century and so was a contemporary of a number of better-known authors of the time who wrote in Greek: Athanasius of Alexandria (who died in the same year as Ephrem, 373), and the Cappadocians, Gregory of Nazianzus, Basil of Caesarea and his brother Gregory of Nyssa. Ephrem came from Nisibis, somewhat further east and on the border between the Roman and Persian Empires (modern Nuseybin in eastern Turkey, on the border now with Syria). Most of his life was spent in Nisibis, serving as a deacon in a church whose building still stands. In 363, however, Nisibis was handed over in a peace treaty to the Persian Empire, and Ephrem became a refugee, ending up in Edessa (modern Şanliurfa), some 100 kilometres to the west. Few genuine details of his life are known, but one thing that evidently impressed later generations was the fact that he introduced women's choirs to sing his hymns.

Besides Ephrem, the only other poet included here whose name is known is Jacob of Serugh (to the southwest of Edessa), who lived a century and a half later. Jacob, who ended up as bishop of Serugh for the last few years of his life (he died in 521), had a wonderful gift for composing verse homilies (a distinctive Syriac genre), of which several hundred survive. These are for the most part highly imaginative re-presentations of biblical episodes, showing great insight in his understanding of the spiritual meaning of the biblical text.

The authors of a large number of the poems in this collection remain unknown; it is likely that most of them will have belonged to the fifth or sixth century, though at least two (Ch. III, no. 1; Ch. IV, no. 12), on stylistic grounds, are likely to belong to the Middle Ages.

The poems included in this collection take three different forms, lyric, narrative, and dialogue. The majority of the lyric poems (or hymns) are by Ephrem, this being his favoured medium; they employ a variety of often quite elaborate metres (Syriac poetry is syllabic in character), though in any one poem the same metre is employed throughout. These stanzaic poems were sung, and the melody titles survive, though the melodies themselves do not.

Ephrem also wrote some narrative poems, using seven-syllable couplets, and one of these is represented here (Ch. IV, no. 7, on the Sinful Woman of Luke 7). Since this particular metre was known by Ephrem's name, many poems using it came to be falsely attributed to him: this applies to all the other narrative poems in this metre included in this collection (Ch. III, nos. 7 and 12; Ch. IV, nos. 4 and 5). A different metre, using twelve-syllable couplets, was the normal one used by Jacob of Serugh (and hence is known by his name): Jacob's poem on Tamar (Ch. III, no. 8) is accordingly in this metre.

The dialogue poems represent a distinctive Syriac genre, whose roots go back to Ancient Mesopotamia: there the dialogues took the form of precedence disputes, and this is still the case in some poems by Ephrem where Satan and Death are the protagonists. In most of the dialogue poems in Syriac, however, the starting point is a moment of tension, potential or actual, in the biblical text, and the speakers (normally two) conduct an argument in alternating verses, employing a simple syllabic metre. Normally there is also an alphabetic acrostic present, commencing with the dialogue proper. Despite being highly stylized in character, these dialogue poems can also be very realistic (as in Mary and Joseph), and sometimes a certain sense of humour is also present, though underlying all this there are serious theological issues, such as the conflict of faith versus reason, which are raised.[2] Their original liturgical context was in the Night Office (where their lively content may have helped to dispel drowsiness!); those translated here belong either to the season of Nativity–Epiphany or to Holy Week.

These three different genres allow for three very different approaches to the biblical text.[3] Accordingly, in a few cases, examples of two different approaches to the same topic have been juxtaposed in order to bring this out (Ch. III, nos. 6 and 7; Ch. IV, nos. 3, 4, 7 and 8). In Ephrem's lyrical poems the biblical characters have the appearance of belonging simultaneously to the past and to the present, not being anchored in either time or space. Thus, in Ephrem's hymn on the Nativity (Ch. V, no. 2), where Mary is certainly the speaker of the opening verses, and is very probably also the voice of the rest of the poem, she starts out addressing her infant son in the cradle, but later on the people whom she is addressing are Ephrem's contemporaries—or indeed, ours, his modern readers. Furthermore, at the end of the poem she is also conveying theological teaching highly relevant to the controversies of Ephrem's own time: in effect, she is being presented here as Ephrem's own spokesperson.

[2] A listing of the surviving Syriac dialogues can be found in my "Syriac dispute poems: the various types," in G.J. Reinink and H.L.J. Vanstiphout (eds), *Dispute Poems and Dialogues in the Ancient and Medieval Near East* (Orientalia Lovaniensia Analecta 42; Leuven, 1991), pp. 109–19 (reprinted in *From Ephrem to Romanos: Interactions between Syriac and Greek in Late Antiquity* (Aldershot, 1999), Ch. VII, with Addenda, pp. 4–5).

[3] This aspect is well brought out by S.A. Harvey in her essay "On Mary's voice: gendered words in Syriac Marian tradition," in D.B. Martin and P. Cox Miller (eds), *The Cultural Turn in Late Ancient Studies* (Durham NC/London, 2005), pp. 63–86.

The narrative poems provide the opportunity for imaginative retellings of the biblical narrative. In the anonymous poems these occur without any overt homiletic elements, whereas in Jacob's poems the homiletic aspect is prominent, and the standard English description of them as "verse homilies" is entirely appropriate. Although great use is made of direct speech, there is much more of a sense of distance between the biblical characters and the poet (and his audience) than is the case with Ephrem's poems.

The dialogues usually take their starting point from a moment of tension in the biblical text, and this is explored by means of the dialogue. In one of the most moving of these, that on the Sinful Woman and Satan (Ch. IV, no. 8), the poet brings out into the open, through the character of Satan, the hesitation and uncertainty that he imagines must have been in the woman's mind in deciding whether or not to risk going into a complete stranger's house and boldly anointing the feet of a guest there.

There are a number of recurrent themes and images that are found in the texts translated in this collection, not all of which will be familiar. Here attention might be drawn to a few of these.[4] Syriac authors often have a liking for using imagery from everyday life, and in particular that of putting on and taking off one's clothes. The metaphor of "putting on" is of course a familiar one from the Bible, and Paul makes considerable use of it, most notably the phrase "to put on Christ" (Rom 13.14). But it is among Syriac writers that one encounters clothing imagery most consistently used in a theological context.[5] When early Syriac writers wished to express the Greek verb used for the incarnation, *esarkōthē*, "he was enfleshed," they regularly employed the phrase "he put on the body." This happened to fit

[4]An excellent introduction to the imagery used in early Syriac writers is provided by R. Murray, *Symbols of Church and Kingdom: A Study in Early Syriac Tradition* (2nd edn, London/Piscataway NJ, 2004).

[5]Some further details on this theme can be found in my "The Robe of Glory: a biblical image in the Syriac tradition," in *Spirituality and Clothing = The Way* 39 (1999), pp. 247–59.

well with the imagery of the "garment of glory" (or "praise") which they inherited from the Jewish background of Syriac Christianity. This "garment of glory" features in the Book of Enoch as the raiment of the Just at the end of time; equally, according to an early Jewish interpretation of Genesis 3.21, this was the clothing of Adam and Eve before the Fall: instead of the usual understanding of the verse, that God made garments of skin for Adam and Eve *after* the Fall, the verb was taken as a pluperfect, thus referring to *before* the Fall, and the garments were not of "skin" (*'wr* in Hebrew), but of "light" (*'wr*) or of "glory." Thanks to this understanding, it was now possible to describe the whole course of salvation history in terms of clothing imagery, with the divine drama occurring in five scenes:

Scene 1: Adam and Eve are clothed in a garment of glory in Paradise before the Fall.

Scene 2: At the Fall they are stripped of this garment, and become aware of their nakedness. From this point on, the divine purpose is to reclothe humanity (represented by Adam and Eve), while at the same time allowing them to exercise fully the divine gift of free will. In the Old Testament God "puts on (human) terms," letting himself be described in human language in order to bring human beings to knowledge of himself and of his purpose for humanity.

Scene 3: At the incarnation the Son "put on the body," and at his Baptism in the Jordan he deposits the garment of glory in the river, so that it becomes once again available for human beings to put on.

Scene 4: At Christian Baptism the individual Christian puts on, in potential, this garment of glory, since the sanctification of the baptismal water has accorded to that water the potency of the Jordan's water in which Christ was baptized.

Scene 5: At the last judgement the righteous will find themselves wearing this raiment of glory/praise in reality.

In order to bring out the relationship between the "potential" of
scene 4 and the "reality" of scene 5, the imagery is connected with
the parable of the Wedding Garment in Matthew 22.1–12. Unlike
modern usage (except sometimes for bridesmaids) where wedding
guests have to provide their own clothing, in antiquity there was also
a custom of providing the guests with garments beforehand, which
of course makes much better sense of the parable, for the man who
is thrown out for not having a wedding garment (Matthew 22.11–12)
has evidently soiled, lost, or sold the one he had previously been
given. Linked with this understanding is the view that Baptism
corresponds to betrothal, and the *eschaton*, or end of time, with the
actual wedding feast.

Closely associated with all this is the concep of Christ as Bridegroom. On the paradigmatic and collective level it is the Church
who is the bride, but on the individual level it is the soul of each
baptized Christian, so that Baptism is in a very dramatic sense
also a betrothal. This idea is by no means confined to Syriac writers, for it can equally be found in some Greek and Latin Fathers;
John Chrysostom's baptismal homilies, for example, abound in
wedding imagery. Syriac authors, however, were able to bring out
the implications of the imagery even more dramatically, thanks
to a variant reading at Matthew 25.10 which was widely known.
At the end of the parable of the Wise and Foolish Virgins, in the
standard Syriac biblical text and in the Greek original, when the
Bridegroom comes, the Wise Virgins enter the Wedding Ban-
quet. According to the variant reading, however, they enter the
"Bridal Chamber," implying a much more intimate scenario. It
is a remarkable fact that if one looks through almost any Syriac
liturgical texts, one will discover that the term which is most
commonly encountered for the kingdom of heaven is "the Bridal
Chamber," usually with the added "of light" or "of joys." Numerous

examples of this clothing and bridal imagery will be found in the course of the texts collected here.[6]

A very important term, especially in the early Syriac writers, is *rāzā*, "mystery, hidden secret, symbol." In the plural, *rāzē*, the term is a standard one for the eucharistic Mysteries (as *ta Mystēria* in Greek), but in a biblical context the word is often most helpfully translated by "symbol," that is, a pointer to a greater reality. It is important to realize, however, that "symbol" is used here in a strong sense, in that the symbol actually participates in some sense in the reality: there is a "hidden power," or "meaning," that links the two. This is, of course, very different from the more widespread understanding of the term today, where a symbol is essentially something different from the reality it points to. For Syriac authors, and for the Fathers in general, it could be said that the symbol is enhanced and validated by the reality it points to.

These *rāzē* are understood as being latent both in the natural world and in the biblical text. Once they are perceived, they can function either horizontally, as it were travelling in historical time from the Old Testament to the New Testament, or to the life of the Church; or they can travel vertically, in sacred time, from this world to the heavenly world. In each case they point to a different aspect of an objective divine reality. For Ephrem (and the Fathers in general), the hermeneutical key to these *rāzē* is provided by Christ himself: it is he who gives proper meaning to them. Thus, for example, difficult Old Testament passages, such as Genesis 22 and 38 (to take two examples covered in Ch. III below), suddenly "make sense" when seen as *rāzē* pointing forward to Christ. *How* these *rāzē*, latent everywhere, can be perceived, according to Ephrem, will emerge in the course of the next chapter.

---

[6]The imagery of the Bridal Chamber is discussed in my "The Bridal Chamber of Light: a distinctive feature of the Syriac liturgical tradition," *The Harp* (Kottayam) 18 (2005), pp. 179–91.

Finally, a few words should be said about the Syriac Bible. The official Syriac biblical text of all the Churches of Syriac tradition is known as the Peshitta, or "straightforward" version, a name devised only in about the eighth century in order to distinguish it from much more literal translations of both the Old and New Testament made from the Greek in the seventh century.

The Syriac Old Testament was translated from Hebrew, while the so-called "apocrypha," or deutero-canonical books, were translated from Greek—with one exception, Ecclesiasticus, or Ben Sira (in Syriac, Bar (A)sira, as will emerge from Ch. IV, no. 4), which was done from Hebrew. For the most part, the text of the Peshitta Old Testament follows the present Hebrew text closely, much more so than that of the Septuagint, where some books were translated from a lost different edition (a notable case is Jeremiah). In certain books the Syriac translators were clearly aware of exegetical traditions and phraseology that are also known from the Jewish Targumim or elsewhere; one instance of this is to be found in Ch. III, no. 6.

The Peshitta New Testament was translated from Greek, but it has a shorter canon than the Greek New Testament (followed by the Vulgate and modern translations), for it lacks 2 Peter, 2–3 John, Jude and the Apocalypse, although these books were subsequently translated and to some extent used. The Peshitta Gospels were in fact a revision of an earlier text known as the "Old Syriac" (which survives independently in two incomplete manuscripts), while the earliest Syriac Gospel text seems to have been Tatian's Diatessaron, or Harmony of the Four Gospels. Although Ephrem wrote a Commentary on this in the fourth century, some fifty or so years later it was actively suppressed, and so no longer survives in its original form. The Diatessaron nevertheless left its mark, especially in liturgical poetry, where a number of characteristic terms can be traced back to it.

Ephrem on Reading Scripture

Even in the case of those religions, notably Judaism, Christianity and Islam, which have a sacred book, or books, that are regarded as the Word of God, or as having been produced under some form of inspiration, the text of these sacred books is often difficult to understand, and so requires interpretation on the part of the hearer and reader. These difficulties may be due to obscurities of language and syntax, or to the presence of different passages which have the appearance of giving contradictory statements within the corpus as a whole. This being so, much will depend on the human interpretation of these Scriptures, and as both history and contemporary experience amply show, different people can extract very different meanings from exactly the same texts. Accordingly it is essential to know how a sacred text should be approached, if it is to function properly as conveying aspects of divine truth and God's message to humanity. Several of the early Church Fathers thought deeply about this matter and can offer sound advice that remains as valuable today as it was for their contemporaries. One of those who have left in writing some of their thoughts on the subject was the Syriac poet Ephrem.

Besides being an outstanding poet, Ephrem was also a theologian of great profundity, although he never presents his theological vision all together in any single work.[1] Instead, he leaves it to the reader to discover this, gradually perceiving that its structure in fact forms an invisible skeleton behind the outward body of his poetry. As vehicles for conveying his theology Ephrem never employs the carefully

[1] An outline of Ephrem's theological vision is attempted in my *The Luminous Eye: the Spiritual World Vision of St Ephrem* (Kalamazoo, 1992).

defined technical terms of a more analytical approach to theology; he uses instead the symbol (*rāzā*) and paradox, since these invite contemplative thought.[2] As the philosopher Paul Ricoeur put it, "La symbole donne à penser." Ephrem's concern is with a non-discursive truth that cannot be empirically verified, but that is, nevertheless, capable of being experienced, given the right approach.

In what follows, some of the main passages where he talks about how to interpret the Bible and gain a proper understanding of its text are collected together and presented.

Ephrem frequently speaks of the "chasm" that exists between God and creation. Since this chasm cannot be crossed by human beings, God would be completely unknowable if he did not choose to reveal himself by crossing over the chasm and thus making himself available, as it were, to human knowledge. The two means by which God thus reveals himself to human beings are the natural world and the biblical text. Ephrem speaks of these as God's two "witnesses":

> In his book Moses
>   described the creation of the natural world
> so that both Nature and Scripture
>   might testify to the Creator:
> Nature, through man's use of it,
>   Scripture, through his reading of it.
> They are witnesses which reach everywhere;
>   they are to be found at all times,
> present at every hour,
>   rebuking the unbeliever
>   who denies the Creator.
>
>   (Hymns on Paradise, 5:2)

Since God has endowed human beings with free will, the revelation of himself is not imposed on them:

[2]An excellent introduction is to be found in R. Murray's "The theory of symbolism in St Ephrem's theology," in *Parole de l'Orient* 6/7 (1975/6), pp. 1–20.

> Any kind of adornment that is the result of compulsion
> is not genuine, for it is merely imposed:
> herein lies the greatness of God's gift,
> that a person can adorn themselves of their own accord,
> in that God has removed all compulsion.
>> (Nisibene Hymns, 16:11)

In order to allow to human beings a freedom of response, God reveals himself indirectly through the *rāzē*, "symbols, mysteries," which are latent everywhere in both Nature and Scripture: Ephrem exclaims,

> Lord, your symbols are everywhere,
> yet you are hidden from everywhere!
>> (Hymns on Faith, 4:9)

In order to begin to perceive these symbols, however, one needs to respond in the right frame of mind:

> Your fountain is hidden from the person who does not
>> thirst for you;
> your treasury seems empty to the person who rejects you.
> Love is the treasurer of your heavenly treasure store.
>> (Hymns on Faith, 32:3)

Elsewhere Ephrem explains how symbols are perceived by using as an analogy the way the eye sees. According to a widespread understanding of his time, the more the eye is filled with light, the more it is enabled to see. The interior eye of the mind or heart is described by Ephrem as operating in the same sort of manner, but instead of light, it is now faith which enables this inner eye to see. Furthermore, this inner eye must itself be pure from sin. Provided these conditions are met, a person will be enabled to perceive the *rāzē*, symbols, hidden in Nature and Scripture, and the greater the faith, the more *rāzē* that person will see.

> The Scriptures are laid out like a mirror,
> and the person whose inner eye is pure
> sees therein the image of Divine Reality.
>
> (Hymns on Faith, 67:8)

Thus the way to perceiving God's self-revelation in this world—and thus the way to any genuine knowledge of God—depends on human response and choice, in other words, the exercise of free will. In Ephrem's view, a purification of the inner eye of faith, combined with a loving yearning for the divine truth, are the two essential prerequisites for a proper perception of the *rāzē* in the biblical text: since these conditions can only be reached through the right exercise of the gift to human beings of free will, Ephrem can say

> the volition of our free will is the key to your treasure.
>
> (Hymns on the Church, 13:5)

One means of God's self-revelation in the Bible is through his allowing himself to be described in human terms. At one point Ephrem humorously compares God's way of instructing humanity to a person who is trying to teach a parrot to speak, using a mirror: it is only by presenting the parrot with a reflection of itself that it will try to imitate human speech. In this case, of course, both the human trainer and the parrot are each part of the created world, so God's stooping to the human level is in fact far more dramatic.

> Let us give thanks to God who has clothed himself
>   in the names of the body's various parts:
> Scripture refers to his "ears"—to teach that he listens to us;
>   it speaks of his "eyes"—to show that he sees us.
> It was just the names of such things that he put on,
>   and although in his true Being there is no "wrath" or
>   "regret,"
> yet he put on these names too because of our weakness.

We should realize that, had he not put on the names of
    such things,
    it would not have been possible for him
to speak with us humans. By means of what belongs to us
    did he draw close to us: he has clothed himself in our
    language,
so that he might clothe us in his mode of life.
    He asked for our form, and put this on,
and then, as a father with his children, he spoke with our
    childish state.

It is our terms that he put on—though he did not literally
    do so;
    he then took them off—without actually doing so:
when wearing them, he was at the same time stripped of
    them.
    He puts on one when it is beneficial, then strips it off in
    exchange for another.
The fact that he strips off and puts on all sorts of terms
    tells us that the term does not apply to his true Being:
because that Being is hidden, he has depicted it by means
    of what is visible. . . .

For this is the Good One, who could have forced us to
    please him,
    without any trouble to himself; but instead, he toiled
    by every means
so that we might act pleasingly to him of our own free will,
    so that we might depict our beauty
with the colours that our own free will had gathered;
    whereas, if he had adorned us, it would have resembled
a portrait that someone else had painted, adorning it with
    his own colours.

A person who is teaching a parrot to speak
    hides behind a mirror and teaches it in this way:
when the bird turns in the direction of the voice which is
    speaking,
    it finds in front of its eyes its own resemblance reflected;
it imagines that it is another parrot, conversing with itself.
    The man puts the bird's image in front of it,
so that by this means it might learn how to speak.

This bird is a fellow creature with the man,
    but although this relationship exists, the man beguiles
    and teaches
the parrot something alien to itself by means of itself;
    in this way he speaks with it.
The Divine Being, who in all things is exalted above all
    things,
    in his love bent down from on high and acquired from
    us what we are used to:
he has labored by every means so as to turn all to himself.
                    (Hymns on Faith, 31:1–3, 5–7)

Accordingly, Ephrem is emphatic that too literal an understanding
of the biblical text is not only going to result in a misunderstanding,
but it is also abusing God's condescension in abasing himself to a
level which human beings are able to comprehend:

If someone concentrates their attention
    solely on the metaphors used of God's majesty,
that person abuses and misrepresents his majesty
    and thus goes astray
by means of those same metaphors
    with which God has clothed himself for that person's
    benefit,

> and he is ungrateful to that Grace
>> which stooped low
> to the level of his childishness,
>> and although Grace has nothing in common with him,
> She clothed herself in his likeness
>> in order to bring him to the likeness of herself.
>
> (Hymns on Paradise, 11:6)

Ephrem speaks of two different approaches to the interpretation of the Biblical text; these he calls "factual" and "spiritual." The former corresponds approximately to a historical and academic approach of today, where (in theory at least) it is possible to speak of correct or erroneous interpretations since, in the search for what is "factual," two different interpretations cannot both at the same time be correct. By contrast, where the "spiritual" meaning is concerned, it is not a case of either/or, but of both/and, since it is possible for many different meanings all to have validity at the same time: they represent different perspectives on the divine reality that lies behind the text. In Ephrem's terminology, a single verse may contain many different *rāzē*, but they are all pointers to the same *shrara*, "truth," that is divine reality. Thus, as far as the biblical text's outer, or "factual," meaning is concerned, this remains univalent, whereas from the point of view of its inner, or "spiritual" meaning, it is multivalent. Speaking of the inner meaning, Ephrem writes:

> If there only existed a single sense for the words of Scripture, then the first commentator to come along would discover it, and other hearers would experience neither the labor of searching, nor the joy of finding. Rather, each word of our Lord has its own form, and each form has its own members, and each member has its own character. Each individual understands it according to his capacity and interprets it as it is granted him.
>
> (Commentary on the Diatessaron, 7:22)

For Ephrem, any search for the spiritual meaning of the biblical text will involve an interaction between the text and the reader (or hearer): the former was written under the inspiration of the Holy Spirit, and the latter needs to be open to the ongoing inspiration of the same Spirit: it needs to be a work of cooperation and interaction, where the reader/hearer needs to "thirst" and to approach with a sense of love. This need for a right approach, with openness and a purity of heart, is important, since a wrong approach will be in serious danger of ending up with a complete misinterpretation of the biblical text. But even when a right approach is present, it will be found that the same text may offer different spiritual meanings to different people, and indeed to the same person on different occasions. As Ephrem points out in another passage from his Commentary on the Diatessaron, latent in the biblical text is an inexhaustible fountain of spiritual meanings:

> Who is capable of comprehending the extent of what is to be discovered in a single utterance of yours? For we leave behind in it far more than we take from it, like thirsty people drinking from a fountain. The facets of his words are more numerous that the faces of those who learn from them. God has depicted his words with many beauties, so that each of those who learn from them can examine that aspect of them which he likes. And God has hidden within his words all sorts of treasures, so that each of us can be enriched by them from whatever aspects they meditate on. For God's word is the Tree of Life which proffers blessed fruits to you on all sides; it is like the Rock which was struck in the Wilderness, which became a spiritual drink for everyone on all sides: "They ate the food of the Spirit and they drank the draft of the Spirit" (1 Corinthians 10.3).
>
> Anyone who encounters Scripture should not suppose that the single one of its riches that he has found is the only one to exist; rather, he should realize that he himself is only

capable of discovering that one out of the many riches which exist in it. Nor, because Scripture has enriched him, should the reader impoverish it. Rather, if the reader is incapable of finding more, let him acknowledge Scripture's magnitude. Rejoice because you have found satisfaction, and do not be grieved that there has been something left over by you. A thirsty person rejoices because he has drunk; he is not grieved because he proved incapable of drinking the fountain dry. Let the fountain vanquish your thirst; your thirst should not vanquish the fountain! If your thirst comes to an end while the fountain has not been diminished, then you can drink again whenever you are thirsty; whereas, if the fountain had been drained dry once you have had your fill, your victory over it would have proved to your own harm! Give thanks for what you have taken away, and do not complain about the superfluity that is left over. What you have taken off with you is your portion; what has been left behind can still be your inheritance.

(Commentary on the Diatessaron 1:18–19)

For Ephrem, both the fundamentalist and the rationalist approaches to the Bible are equally unsatisfactory and arrogant, each in its own different way: by concentrating their attention on the literal or historical meaning, they neglect another dimension, capable of much more profound meaning, which lies hidden beneath the surface meaning of the biblical text. "Do not merely ask the meaning of the words," he writes, "for these, taken in their outward sense, can impede the real point; rather, search out their true sense and what they really refer to" (Commentary on the Diatessaron 22:3).

Ephrem's distinction between the two different kinds of interpretation remains of fundamental importance. Whereas with the factual approach there is the possibility of discovering a single correct interpretation, which then imposes itself and rules out all others, with the spiritual approach, many different interpretations can exist simultaneously, but they cannot impose themselves. With the former it is a case of an objective meaning that is univalent, but with the latter the meaning is polyvalent but remains subjective (though the reality of which it is a subjective experience is an objective divine reality). The two modes of interpretation ought to be seen as complementary, and it is only when the one or the other makes claims that trespass, as it were, on the other's territory that things go wrong and the spectre of a supposed conflict between the two arises.

The Old Testament

1. The rivers Pishon and Jordan (Genesis 2.11; Matthew 3.13): anonymous dialogue poem

Introduction

When Johann Sebastian Bach wrote his Cantata on the contest of the Four Rivers (BWV 206) it is totally unlikely that he would have been aware of the playful Syriac poem on the contest of the rivers Pishon and Jordan, which opens this chapter. The Pishon is the first of the four rivers flowing out of Paradise that are mentioned in Genesis 2.11–14. The idea of a dispute with the river Jordan might have been suggested by Naaman's derisive remark when told to wash in the Jordan, "Are not Abana and Pharpar, the rivers of Damascus, better than all the waters of Israel?" (2 Kings 5.12). Though Naaman's cleansing in the Jordan from leprosy does not specifically get mentioned here, there is a passing allusion in the first stanza, and in any case the episode was widely considered as a type for Christian Baptism, and there are several allusions to the Jordan's role as a fountainhead of Christian Baptism, as well as the river in which Christ was baptized (see also Ch. V, no. 3). The liturgical setting of the poem is, appropriately, Epiphany, with (in all the Eastern Christian rites) its blessing of the water, which is alluded to in stanza 23. Although it is preserved only in a late nineteenth-century manuscript, it represents a genuine precedence dispute, of the type that is familiar from Ancient Mesopotamia.

Translation

1. Blessed is the Lord of all rivers
    who left aside all other rivers
    to choose the Jordan, smallest of rivers,   2 Kg 5.12
    to adorn it with every kind of beauty.

2. PISHON: The Pishon in envy says,
    "My course is more beloved than the Jordan's";
    to which the enviable Jordan replied
    with deeds and not with words:

3. JORDAN: In what way is your land better
    or your course more beloved?
    Come, stand in the Court of Truth
    with deeds and not with words.

4. PISHON: I am chosen since I issue from Eden,   Gen 2.10–11
    and I am full of gold and of jacynths.   Gen 2.12
    I am remembered in the presence of all kings,
    with deeds and not with words.

5. JORDAN: Though you issue from Eden, as you have said,
    and are full of gold and of jacynths,
    yet compared to my greatness you are small
    in deeds, though not in words.

6. PISHON: Look how my precious stones rest upon the head
            of every king
    and on the face of every princess,
    adorning all their hands—
    with deeds and not with words.

7. JORDAN: You should realize that your beauty
    has caused humanity to inherit all that is ugly,

whereas in me it has acquired the baptismal bath of
    purity,   Titus 3.5
in deed and not just in word.

8. PISHON: I provide beauty and radiance,
    I am full of treasures of pearls.
    How can you say that I am rejected
    in deeds rather than in words?

9. JORDAN: Look how they pass away, those beauties that you
    provide;
    the treasuries you fill will become deficient,
    whereas my waves will give benefit, and not cause loss
    in deeds rather than in words.

10. PISHON: My precious stones and beryls are better,
    my waves are mightier than yours.
    How is it that you act so proudly against me
    in deeds and not just in words?

11. JORDAN: The sea of Okeanos is greater than you -
    maybe it is your source;
    but your Lord and mine has made me greater than you
    in deeds, if not in words.

12. PISHON: Though I issue from the Okeanos,
    yet it is from the Sea of Tiberias that you come;
    and I am full of crystal
    —in deed and not just in word.

13. JORDAN: Your gems have made into harlots
    both free-born women and true,
    whereas in me they have put on chastity
    in deed and not just in word.

14. PISHON: Why do you mention harlots?
    Call to mind the kings and queens
    who in their very sleep yearn to behold me
    in deed and not just in word.

15. JORDAN: It is foolish souls,
    and not the virtuous, who yearn for you:
    your beauties end up in sorrows
    —in deed, and not just in word.

16. PISHON: A great many are the sorrows
    of those who have received nothing from me,
    whereas for those who enter me there are joys
    in deed and not just in word.

17. JORDAN: It is toil they inherit, those who enter you,
    and those who leave you acquire pain in abundance;
    then, like cattle, they finally die
    —in deed, and not just in word.

18. PISHON: I am very special, seeing that I issue from Eden,

    Gen 2.10–11

    the blessed land, pure and holy,
    whereas you are from Jericho, the accursed

    Josh 6.26, 1 Kg 16.34

    in deed and not only in word.

19. JORDAN: To Jericho you shall not come,
    but to your Lord, come, let us go,
    and let us each bring all that we have
    in deed and not just in word.

20. PISHON: "Arise, Euphrates and Tigris," cried the Pishon,

    Gen 2.13–14

    "I too am with you, O Gihon:

the Jordan has insulted me and you
in deed and not just in word."

21. JORDAN: Tens of thousands have drowned in all of you,
    myriads of sins have been performed in you,
    whereas in me you have all received sanctification
    in deed and not just in word.

22. JORDAN: In me did the Only-Begotten Son reside,
    over me was the exalted Father revealed,
    upon me did the living Spirit descend   Mt 3.16–17 and par.
    in deed and not just in word.

23. JORDAN: In me have all debts been cancelled,   Col 2.14
    in me all those baptized receive salvation,
    in me all fountains are blessed
    —in deed and not just in word.

24. The seas and rivers grew weak
    as astonishment fell upon them,
    and victory was the Jordan's
    in deed and not just in word.

25. Praise to the Divinity
    at the Union with the Humanity,
    and on the author of this poem
    be mercy—and equally upon us as well.

2. Paradise described (Genesis 2–3):
Ephrem, Hymns on Paradise, 2

Introduction (to Hymns on Paradise, 2 and 3)

The Paradise narrative in Genesis 1–3 has always been seen in Christianity as providing a description of how humanity came to be in what is observably a fallen state. For Ephrem, Adam and Eve represent humanity: "with Adam, we too left Paradise," he exclaims. His explanation of the nature of the Fall and how it happened[1] is considerably different from that familiar from much of western Christian tradition: in his view, Adam and Eve/humanity were created in an intermediate state, neither mortal, nor immortal: how they would end up depended on the exercise of their free will, and in particular, whether they would obey God's "tiny commandment" not to eat of one particular tree, God's intention in giving this commandment to them being to give them the opportunity to win the reward of immortality through their own right choice. Their failure to keep the commandment results in their fall into the state of mortality, in which they lose the "garment of glory" in which they had been created. The whole aim of God's subsequent plan of salvation is to reclothe humanity in this primordial garment of glory (whose origin lies in a Jewish exegetical tradition) and return it, not to primordial paradise, but to the eschatological paradise where there will be access to the Tree of Life (also identified with Christ himself).

Ephrem wrote a cycle of fifteen poems on Paradise. In many ways these could be described as meditations on different aspects of it. At one point he describes his experience of reading the Genesis narrative:

---

[1]This is set out very clearly in his Commentary on Genesis, the relevant sections of which can be found translated in my *St Ephrem the Syrian, Hymns on Paradise* (Crestwood, NY, 1990), pp. 197–224.

> I read the opening of this book
>   and was filled with joy,
> for its verses and lines
>   spread out their arms to welcome me;
> the first rushed out and kissed me,
>   and led me on to its companion
> wherein is written
>   the story of Paradise;
> it lifted me up and transported me
>   from the bosom of the book
> to the very bosom of Paradise.
>
> The eye and the mind
>   travelled over the lines
> as over a bridge, and entered together
>   the story of Paradise.
> The eye as it read
>   transported the mind;
> in return, the mind too
>   gave the eye rest
> from its reading,
>   for when the book had been read
> the eye had rest,
>   but the mind was engaged (5:3–4).

For Ephrem, as for Dante, Paradise was a mountain (based on Ezekiel 28.13–14, rather than Genesis). Although Paradise is not part of the geography of this world, it is somehow connected with it: to indicate this Ephrem visualises it as a cone whose base circumference went around the ocean that was thought to encircle the world. In the two poems translated below Ephrem turns to the eschatological aspect of Paradise, the key to whose door lies in conduct on earth, seeing that Paradise itself is able to discern between the good and the bad, and lets in only those whose lives conform to its own beauty. Furthermore, the different levels on the Paradise mountain are reserved for different categories of the just, and correspond to the different storeys in the Ark and the different levels on Mount Sinai at the Lawgiving. Right at the end of the first of the two hymns translated here Ephrem reveals that, while the arrangements in the Ark and on Sinai serve to illustrate the situation in Paradise, Paradise itself is a depiction of the Church: in other words (though this is not stated explicitly here), the Church potentially anticipates the eschatological Paradise, the Tree of Life being Christ who makes himself present in the Eucharist.

In the next hymn Ephrem tells how the Tree of Life, situated at the summit of the mountain, had been hidden from Adam and Eve by the Tree of the Knowledge of Good and Evil, whose fruit they had been forbidden; this was situated in the middle of Paradise and served as a boundary, fencing off the "sanctuary" from the "Holy of Holies," of whose very existence Adam was unaware. As a result of their disobedience Adam and Eve became aware of two things: the existence of a higher state for which they had been destined, but which they had lost, and an awareness that they were now stripped naked of their former glory. Adam's act of presumption was similar to that of King Uzziah who tried to usurp a role that was not his by entering the temple to burn incense (2 Chr 26.16).

Translation

1. Blessed is the person
          for whom Paradise yearns.
    Yes, Paradise yearns for that person whose goodness
          makes them beautiful:
    it engulfs them at its gateway;
          it embraces them in its bosom;
    it caresses them in its very womb,
          for it splits open and receives them

into its inmost parts.
    But if there is someone it abhors,
it removes him and casts him out.
    This is the gate of testing
that belongs to him who loves mankind.

(Response) Blessed is he who was pierced   Jn 19.34
    and so removed the sword from the entry to
    Paradise!   Gen 3.24

2. Forge here on earth and take
        the key to Paradise:
    the Door that welcomes you   cf. Jn 10.9
        smiles radiantly upon you;
    the Door, all discerning,
        conforms its measurements to those who enter it:
    in its wisdom
        it shrinks and grows.
    According to the stature and rank
        attained by each person,
    it shows by its dimensions
        whether they are perfect, or lacking in something.

3. When people see
        that they have lost everything,
    that riches do not endure
        and carnal lusts no longer exist,
    that beauty and power
        disappear and vanish.
    then they recollect themselves
        and are filled with remorse,
    because, choked with care,
        they heard with contempt those words,

"Your possessions are but a passing dream,
>   your inheritance, darkness."   cf. Mt 8.12; Lk 12.16–20

4. What they once possessed they have lost,
>   and found what they never had;
>   they desired happiness, but it flew away,
>   and the woe they had dreaded has arrived;
>   what they had put their hope on has proved an illusion,
>   and what they had never sought, they have now
>   found.
>   They groan because they have been brought low
>   and have been "robbed,"
>   for their way of life deceived them,
>   while their torment is very real:
>   their luxurious living has vanished,
>   and their punishment does not come to an end.

5. The righteous, too, perceive
>   that their own affliction no longer exists,
>   their suffering does not endure,
>   their burden no longer remains,
>   and it seems as if no anguish
>   had ever assailed them,
>   Their fasts appear
>   as though a mere dream,
>   for they have awoken as if from sleep
>   to discover Paradise
>   and the Kingdom's table   Lk 22.30
>   spread out before them.

6. By those who are outside
>   the summit cannot be scaled,
>   but from inside, Paradise inclines its whole self
>   to all who ascend it.

The whole of its interior
    gazes upon the just with joy.
Paradise girds the loins
    of the world,
encircling the great sea:
    neighbour to the beings on high,
friendly to those within it,
    hostile to those without.

7. At its boundary I saw
    figs, growing in a sheltered place,   Gen 3.7
from which crowns were made that adorned
    the brows of the guilty pair,
while their leaves, as it were, blushed
    for him who was stripped naked:
their leaves were required for those two
    who had lost their garments;
although they covered Adam,
    they still made him blush with shame and repent,
because in a place of such splendour
    a man who is naked is filled with shame.

8. Who is capable of gazing
    upon the Garden's splendour,
seeing how glorious it is in all its design,
    how harmonious in all its proportions,
how spacious for those who dwell there,
    how radiant with its abodes?
Its fountains delight
    with their fragrance,
but when they issue forth towards us   Gen 2.10–14
    they become impoverished in our country,
since they put on the savours of our land
    as we drink them.

9. Indeed, that Will
        for whom everything is easy
    constrains these abundant
        fountains of Paradise,
    confining them with land,
        like water channels;
    he summoned them to issue forth
        in our direction,
    just as he bound up the waters   Prov 30.4
        in the bosom of his clouds,
    ready to be sent forth into the atmosphere
        at the bidding of his Will.

10. When he made this intricate design
        he varied its beauties,
    so that some levels
        were far more glorious than others.
    To the degree that one level
        is higher than another,
    so too is its glory
        the more sublime.
    In this way he allots
        the foothills to the most lowly,
    the slopes to those in between
        and the heights to the exalted.

11. When the just ascend its various levels
        to receive their inheritance,
    with justice he raises up each one
        to the degree that accords with his labors;
    each is stopped at the level
        whereof he is worthy,
    there being sufficient levels in Paradise
        for everyone:

the lowest parts for the repentant,
    the middle for the righteous,
the heights for the victorious,
    while the summit is reserved for God's Presence.[2]

12. Noah made the animals live
        in the lowest part of the Ark;
    in the middle part
        he lodged the birds,
    while Noah himself, like the Deity,
        resided on the upper deck.
    On Mount Sinai it was the people
        who dwelt below,
    the priests round about it,
        and Aaron halfway up,
    while Moses was on its heights
        and the Glorious One on the summit.

13. A symbol of the divisions
        in that Garden of Life
    did Moses trace out in the Ark
        and on Mount Sinai too;
    he depicted for us the types of Paradise
        with all its arrangements:
    harmonious, fair and delectable
        in everything—
    in its height, its beauty,
        its fragrance, and its different species.
    Here is the haven of all riches
        whereby the Church is depicted.

---

[2]Ephrem uses the term Shekhina here.

3. Paradise described (continued):
Ephrem, Hymns on Paradise, 3

Introduction (see above, p. 36)

Translation

1. As for that part of the Garden, my beloved,
        which is situated so gloriously
    at the summit of that height
        where dwells the Glory,
    not even its symbol
        can be depicted in human thought;
    for what mind
        has the sensitivity
    to gaze upon it,
        or the faculties to explore it,
    or the capacity to attain to that Garden
        whose riches are beyond comprehension?

Refrain: Praise to your Justice that crowns the victorious.

2. Perhaps that blessed tree,
        the Tree of Life,   Gen 3.22
    is, by its rays,
        the sun of Paradise;
    its leaves glisten
        and on them are impressed
    the spiritual graces
        of that Garden.
    In the breezes the other trees
        bow down in worship
    before that sovereign
        and leader of the trees.

3. In the very midst he planted
        the Tree of Knowledge,   Gen 2.9
    endowing it with awe,
        hedging it in with dread,
    so that it might straightway serve
        as a boundary to the inner region of Paradise.
    Two things did Adam hear
        in that single decree:
    that they should not eat of it   Gen 2.17
        and that, by shrinking from it,
    they should perceive that it was not lawful
        to penetrate further, beyond that Tree.   Gen 3.7

4. The serpent could not
        enter Paradise,
    for neither animal
        nor bird
    was permitted to approach
        the outer region of Paradise,
    and Adam had to go out
        to meet them,
    so the serpent cunningly learned,
        through questioning Eve,
    the character of Paradise,
        what it was and how it was arranged.

5. When the Accursed One learned
        how the glory of that inner Tabernacle,
    as if in a sanctuary,
        was hidden from them,
    and that the Tree of Knowledge,
        clothed with an injunction,
    served as the veil
        for the sanctuary,

he realized that its fruit
　　was the key of justice
that would open the eyes of the bold
　　—and cause them great remorse.

6.　Their eyes were open—
　　　　though at the same time they were still closed
　　so as not to see the Glory
　　　　or their own low estate;
　　so as not to see the Glory
　　　　of that inner Tabernacle,
　　nor to see the nakedness
　　　　of their own bodies.
　　These two kinds of knowledge
　　　　God hid in the Tree,
　　placing it as a judge
　　　　between the two sides.

7.　But when Adam audaciously ran
　　　　and ate of its fruit,
　　this double knowledge
　　　　straightway flew towards him,
　　tore away and removed
　　　　both veils from his eyes:
　　he beheld the Glory of the Holy of Holies
　　　　and trembled;
　　he beheld, too, his own shame and blushed,
　　　　groaning and lamenting,
　　because the twofold knowledge that he had gained
　　　　had proved for him a torment.

8. Whoever has eaten
        of that fruit
    either sees and is filled with delight,
        or he sees and groans out.
    The serpent incited them to eat in sin,
        so that they might lament;
    having seen the blessed state,
        they could not taste of it—
    like the hero of old
        whose torment was doubled
    because in his hunger he could not taste
        the delights which he beheld.

9. For God had not allowed him
        to see his naked state,
    so that, should he spurn the commandment,
        his ignominy might be shown to him.
    Nor did he show him the Holy of Holies
        in order that, if he kept the commandment,
    he might set eyes upon it
        and rejoice.
    These two things did God conceal
        as the two recompenses,
    so that Adam might receive, by means of his contest,
        a crown that befitted his actions.

10. God established the Tree as judge,
        so that if Adam should eat from it,
    it might show him that rank
        which he had lost through his pride,
    and show him, as well, that low estate
        he had acquired, to his torment.
    Whereas, if he should overcome and conquer,
        it would robe him in glory

and reveal to him also
    the nature of shame,
so that he might acquire, in his good health,
    an understanding of sickness.

11. A person who has acquired
    good health in himself
and is aware in his mind
    of what sickness is,
has gained something beneficial,
    and he knows something profitable;
but the person who lies
    in sickness,
and knows in his mind
    what good health is like,
is vexed by his sickness
    and tormented in his mind.

12. Had Adam conquered,
    he would have acquired
glory upon his limbs,
    and discernment of what suffering is,
so that he might be radiant in his limbs
    and grow in his discernment.
But the serpent reversed all this
    and made him taste
abasement in reality,
    and glory in recollection only,
so that he might feel shame at what he had found
    and weep at what he had lost.

13. The Tree was to him
        like a gate;
    its fruit was the veil
        covering that hidden Tabernacle.
    Adam snatched the fruit,
        casting aside the commandment.
    When he beheld that Glory
        within,
    shining forth with its rays,
        he fled outside;
    he ran off and took refuge
        amongst the modest fig trees.

14. In the midst of Paradise God had planted
        the Tree of Knowledge
    to separate off, above and below,
        Sanctuary from Holy of Holies.
    Adam made bold to touch,
        and he was smitten like Uzziah: 2 Chr 26.20
    the king became leprous;
        Adam was stripped.
    Being struck like Uzziah
        he hastened to leave:
    both kings fled and hid,
        in shame at their bodies.

15. Even though all the trees
        of Paradise
    are clothed each in its own glory,
        yet each veils itself at the Glory:
    the Seraphs with their wings,
        the trees with their branches,
    all cover their faces so as not to behold
        their Lord.

They all blushed at Adam
    who was suddenly found naked;
the serpent had stolen his garments,
    for which it was deprived of its feet.

16. God did not permit
    Adam to enter
that innermost Tabernacle:
    this was withheld,
so that he might first prove pleasing
    in his service of that outer Tabernacle.
Like a priest
    with fragrant incense,
Adam's keeping of the commandment
    was to be his censer;
then he might enter before the Hidden One
    into that hidden Tabernacle.

17. The symbol of Paradise
    was depicted by Moses
who made the two sanctuaries,
    the sanctuary and the Holy of Holies;
into the outer one,
    entrance was permitted,
but into the inner,
    only once a year.   Lev 16.34; Heb 9.7
So too with Paradise,
    God closed off the inner part,
but he opened up the outer,
    wherein Adam might graze.

4. Abel and Cain (Genesis 4.8–12): anonymous dialogue poem

Introduction

Genesis 4 tells of the first murder, and in some exegetical traditions (including the Syriac) Abel is considered to be the first martyr, which of course implies that he died for a cause. The sparse narrative of Genesis 4 leaves many points unresolved, in particular: why was Cain's offering rejected, and how did he know this, why and how did Cain kill Abel? These were matters of great interest to ancient Jewish and Christian exegetes, who provided a variety of different explanations. These, however, are only hinted at in this dialogue poem between the two brothers: it emerges that it was lack of love for God on Cain's part that led to the rejection of his sacrifice (verses 16, 36), and that this rejection was indicated by the divine fire of acceptance descending only on that of his brother (verse 23). The main topic, however, of their argument lies in a different area: Cain has an overweening greed for land, and he cannot bear the idea of sharing ownership of the earth.

The biblical text, of course, does not mention any dialogue between the two brothers, but already in the Jewish Aramaic Targum tradition a dialogue (of a theological nature) has been incorporated, and it is possible that the anonymous Syriac author of the present dialogue poem was aware in a general way of the idea of introducing a dialogue at this point in the biblical narrative.

Translation

1. The story of Abel has filled me with wonder,
    and my mind is reduced to astonishment;
    my tongue is moved to speak
    of that conflict in which the brothers were engaged.

Refrain: O People and Peoples, come, listen and hear
    the story of Abel and Cain:
    cry "Alas for the murderer
    who slew his brother unjustly."

2. The wronged man's blood has silently invited me
    to relate his story so full of grief,
    that even the earth groaned at his blood   Gen 4.10
    when he became the firstborn of that curse.

3. The reason how all this came about
    it is fitting we should relate to those who listen:
    why and how did the brothers quarrel,
    bringing about a murder right from the start.

4. After our father Adam
    had left the Garden, having transgressed,
    he had sons, in accordance with the word
    of the Maker, who so willed it.   Gen 1.28

5. They took on the toil of working the land
    in fulfilment of the judgement which the Just One had
        decreed:
    "With toil and weariness   Gen 3.19, 31.42
    shall you eat bread in the world."

6. Cain took on the labor of the field,   Gen 4.2
    while the upright Abel pastured sheep.
    Adam saw, and was pleased with them,
    receiving comfort after his grief.

7. Adam sat down and summoned his sons;
    they entered and stood before him as he said,
    "From the produce of your work
    offer up firstfruits to the Lord.

8.   Because I sinned he was angry with me
     and drove me from Paradise, casting me out;
     when he is reconciled by your offering,
     then he will turn towards me at your sacrifices."

9.   They carried their offerings, as they were bidden,
     each one bringing from the result of his toil;
     they carried them along to bring to the Lord
     in order to reconcile him–even though he is never angry.

10. Their father Adam waited behind
     to see what would happen to them,
     but the Evil One, full of cunning, attached himself to Cain,
     filling him with anger and wrath.

11. When they reached high ground and the presence of the Lord
     they held out their offerings and presented them.
     With Abel's offering he was pleased,
     but Cain's sacrifice failed to reconcile him.

12. The envious man saw and was clothed in anger;
     down to the valley he dragged his brother.   Gen 4.8
     The Evil One, full of cunning, incited him
     and showed him how to shed blood.

13. CAIN: Says Cain: Since the Lord has taken delight
     in your sacrifice, but rejected mine,   Gen 4.5
     I will kill you: because he has preferred you
     I will get my own back on this his "friend."

14. ABEL: Abel replies: What wrong have I done
     if the Lord has been pleased with me?
     He searches out hearts and so has
             the right   Jer 11.20, Prov 17.3
     to choose or reject as he likes.

15. CAIN: I am the eldest, and so it is right
  that he should accept me, rather than you,
  but he has preferred yours, and mine he has abhorred:
  he has rejected my offering and chosen yours.

16. ABEL: In all offerings that are made
  it is love that he wants to see,
  and if good intention is not mingled in,
  then the sacrifice is ugly and so gets rejected.

17. CAIN: I will deprive you of your Friend,
  for the earth will not hold us both;
  then he will have to accept sacrifice from me,
  when there is no one else beside me.

18. ABEL: Grant me as a favor some small corner
  in the world, and do not kill me.
  The whole world shall be yours,
  then you can offer up your sacrifice just as you like.

19. CAIN: Tears and weeping will not sway me,
  nor will your groans, however plentiful.
  The moment he accepted your sacrifice
  I thought of you as already dead and hidden away.

20. ABEL: You may have this world to yourself,
  but grant me the favor of remaining in it;
  lay the yoke of your rule on my neck,
  but let me have my fill of the life to which I have come.

21. CAIN: From this moment on your mother Eve
  will be deprived of your truth;
  Adam will look for you, but to no avail.
  They will come to consider you as though you had never
   existed.

22. ABEL: Adam will question you about me,
    what answer will you give him?
    His first injury has not yet healed,
    and you will be hitting his wound with thorns.

23. CAIN: If God has sent to accept your offering,
    honouring you greatly with the flames,
    then I will kill you because he has favored you,
    accepting your sacrifice and rejecting mine.

24. ABEL: Alas for my youth, what is become of it,
    seeing that I shall die without having done wrong.
    Show some sorrow, brother, and pity me:
    do not shed my blood, filled with hate.

25. CAIN: Fury has overcome me, and I am filled with anger
    as I go down carrying my offering.
    Why did he not receive it? If you know,
    reveal to me the secret and you will not have to die.

26. ABEL: The mouth is inadequate to relate
    the great vision which I saw there,
    when Truth arose and chose the sacrifice,
    rejecting and selecting just as he wished.

27. CAIN: What profit has it brought you, that vision which you
    saw,
    for it has paved the way for your slaughter and death:
    a robe of suffering has it woven for you, and clothed you in it;
    a garment of blood has it spread out to cover you.

28. ABEL: The vision which I beheld shall deliver me
    from Satan, whose abode you have become.
    If I should die, then both heaven and earth
    are witnesses that I have done no wrong.

29. CAIN: He has clearly selected you and accepted your burnt
       offerings,
    while my offering he has rejected, abhorring my worship.
    So, because he has favoured you,
    I will mix your blood in with your sacrifice.

30. ABEL: He has clearly selected me, just as you say,
    receiving my offering and showing me love.
    See that you do not stain your hands with my blood
    lest he utter some sentence against you.

31. CAIN: A pile of stones will I heap upon you.
    Who will require your blood at my hands?
    We left the Lord behind on the mountain above,
    so who will deliver you if I put you to death?

32. ABEL: That pile of stones which you heap up over me
    will cry out for me, accusing you:
    their clamour shall the Just One hear,
    and he will judge the wrong done to me in accordance with
       his wisdom.

33. CAIN: However much you try to unsettle me,
    my mind's cunning plan will not be wiped out:
    until my hand has tasted of your blood
    I will not stay still or take any rest.

34. ABEL: How heavy my life seems to you
    because the earth will not contain both me and you;
    let my offering count as yours, so be quiet;
    rest from your wrath, and do not kill me.

35. CAIN: He would have accepted me rather than you
    had you not done me this wrong:

you are younger in both age and intelligence,
yet you took first place with the first-fruits.

36. ABEL: He would have chosen you, had you
      acted well,   Gen 4.7
and he would have been pleased with your offering:
you would have been accepted if only you had mixed
sincere love along with your sacrifice.

37. CAIN: What shall I say when Adam asks me
"Why did he not accept you?"
He will be pleased with you—if you remain alive—
but with me he will be angry and treat me as hateful.

38. ABEL: It is an evil death that you will bring upon me,
and Adam will be angry if you kill me.
Spare your mother: let not the young shoot
which sprang from her be cut off.

39. CAIN: That shoot which left me behind, as it went on to grow
      tall,
I will tear out by its roots, lest it hold me back;
with my iciness I will cause it harm, while it is still tender,
lest it grow strong and rebel against me.

40. ABEL: Let your heart be quieted from wrath,
hold yourself back from grief:
look, sin is crouching at the door;   Gen 4.7
do not approach it lest it tear you to pieces.

41. CAIN: He has cast me down and rejected me in anger,
he has refused my offering and abhorred my worship.
What else can he bring against me
more than this if I kill you?

42. ABEL: It is a most cruel thing to shed my blood,
    to destroy the image which his hands have
        fashioned.   Gen 1.27
    Allow the earth to be at peace;
    ask for mercy, and then you will find rest.

43. CAIN: This is a hard thing which you are saying,
    and your words are crueller than the spear:
    after he has shown his dislike, and rebuked me too,
    are you asking me to go and see him face to face?

44. ABEL: O servant who has been fashioned, do not be
        contentious
    towards the Good One who has delineated and adorned you;
    remember the dust from which you came into being,
                                                      Gen 3.19
    and the soil to which you will return.

45. CAIN: Cease from what you are saying:
    you will not escape through talking.
    Your time has come, you wretch,
    it is superfluous for you to be standing there.

46. ABEL: Your heart has been dulled by anger,
    what to say to you I have no idea.
    Let the mountains weep for me from now on,
    seeing that I am going to die in between them.

47. Cain approached his own mother's son and made him kneel
        down
    like a lamb about to be slaughtered.   Is 53.7
    The heights gave a wail, and the depths wept tears
    at the innocent man being slaughtered.

48. The hills bent down to lament
    at this novel corpse in their midst;
    the heavenly ranks were left in stupor
    at what the audacious Cain had done.

49. He cried out in grief as he was bound,
    and the mountains wailed at the sound of his moans;
    the deaf rocks heard his weeping   cf. Mt 27.51
    and gave out a sound in their suffering.

50. The earth cried out when she received
    that first blood that trickled down upon her;
    she gave a thunderous sound at the murderer,
    cursing him as she said, "What have you done?"

51. The elements quaked in terror
    at seeing that first corpse;
    the earth shook as she received
    that first blood that descended upon her.

52. The Lord of all thundered in heaven
    as Abel's blood groaned out before him;   Gen 4.10
    and as Judge he prepared the court,
    summoning Cain, so as to question him.

53. The Father began to question Cain,
    even though he knew very well,
    "Where is your brother? Tell me.   Gen 4.9
    Where has he gone and what happened to him?"

54. Cain heard the Most High
    question him concerning his brother.
    He brazenly lied and said, "I am not aware,
    for I am not Abel's keeper."

55. GOD: "You shall be accursed within the world,　　　Gen 4.11
    and you shall be shaking and trembling there;　　　Gen 4.12
    and every one who shall find you will kill you　　cf. Gen 4.14
    on the earth upon which you have spilt blood."

56. Thanks be to the Exalted who discerningly accepted
    the offering of Abel who had pleased him,
    but rejected the sacrifice of him who is rejected,
    decreeing his judgement in justice.

5. Noah's Ark (Genesis 7–8): Ephrem, Hymns on Faith, 49

Introduction

Noah, like Christ himself, provides the transition between the old order and the new. Thanks to his uprightness, weighty Noah weighs down the scales when he is weighed against his contemporaries: having been lifted up in the scales of justice and so found wanting, they are cast down in the Flood, and it is Noah's turn to be raised up, preserved from the Flood by the Ark. The Ark, which saves him, sails cross-like over the water and serves as a type for the Church, where the water of Baptism is the source of salvation for those who take refuge in her. The dove which announces to Noah that the Flood waters have receded (Gen 8.11) points forward to the Holy Spirit who appeared in the likeness of a dove at the Baptism of Christ (Mt 3.16 and parallels) and who sanctifies the baptismal water in the font, while the olive leaves which Noah's dove carried in its beak look forward to the anointing of the baptismal candidates with olive oil.

The poem has an acrostic giving the first part of Ephrem's own name (the rest is given in the next hymn in the cycle). The self-deprecatory remarks in the last stanza are perhaps deliberately meant to reflect the incomplete acrostic.

Translation

1. How splendid was Noah, whose example surpassed all his
   contemporaries:
   they were weighed in the scales of justice
   and were found wanting;
   a single soul with its armour of chastity
   outbalanced them all.
   They were drowned in the Flood,   Gen 7.23
   having proved too light in the scales,
   while in the Ark
   the chaste and weighty Noah was lifted up.
   Glory be to God who took pleasure in Noah!

Refrain: Praises to your dominion!

2. Noah extended his ministry either side of the Flood,
   depicting two types, sealing up the one that had passed,
   opening up that which followed.
   Between these two generations
   he ministered to two symbols,
   dismissing the former,
   making preparation for the latter.
   He buried the generation grown old,
   and nurtured the youthful one.
   Praises be to him who chose him!

3. Over the Flood the ship of the Lord of all flew,   cf. Gen 7.18
   it left the east, rested in the west,
   flew off to the south,
   and measured out the north;
   its flight over the water
   served as a prophecy for the dry land,
   preaching how its progeny would be
   fruitful in every quarter,

abounding in every region.
Praises to his Savior!

4. The Ark marked out by its course the sign of its Preserver,
   the cross of its Steersman, and the wood of its Sailor
   who has come to fashion for us
   the Church in the waters of Baptism:
   with the threefold name
   he rescues those who reside in her,
   and in the place of the dove,
   the Spirit administers her anointing   Gen 8.11
   and the mystery of her salvation.
   Praises to her Savior!

5. His symbols are in the Law, his types are in the Ark,
   each bears testimony to the other;
   just as the Ark's recesses
   were emptied out, so too the types in Scripture
   were emptied out; for by his coming he embraced
   the symbol of the Law,
   and in his churches he has brought to fulfilment
   the types of the Ark.
   Praise to your coming!

6. My mind wanders, having fallen into the flood
   of our Savior's power.
   Blessed is Noah who,
   through his ship, the Ark,
   floated over the Flood,   Gen 7.18
   yet his mind was recollected.
   May my faith, Lord, be a ship for my weakness,
   since the foolish are drowned
   in the depths of their prying into you.
   Praises be to him who begot you!

6. Abraham and Isaac (Genesis 22): anonymous dialogue poem

Introduction (to 6 and 7)

The stark narrative of Genesis 22, entitled "the testing of Abraham" in the Syriac Bible, has elicited a vast range of different responses in Jewish, Christian and Muslim literature and exegesis, both ancient and modern. For early Christian writers, and for their Jewish contemporaries, the episode is seen as an example of absolute faith and loving trust in God, making the point by presenting the most dramatic and terrible scenario imaginable. Ancient readers will of course have had God's promise of descendants through Isaac (Gen 21.12) in mind, so it is not just a blind faith on Abraham's part, but one based on God's own word: where others would have either despaired or lost trust and rebelled, Abraham's faith in God's promise, even in the most desperate circumstances, holds out. Not for nothing was Abraham called "Friend of God" (Isaiah 41.8, 2 Chronicles 20.7), which continues as his standard title in Islam.

The biblical narrative is so bare that its very silences invite questions, and one question which ancient commentators, Jewish and Christian, asked was "What about Isaac's mother, Sarah?" It was usually assumed that the reason she is not mentioned was because Abraham did not tell her what he was going to do, and a whole range of explanations were suggested for this. It is on this point that Greek and Syriac commentators usually take different stances: whereas Greek authors tend to say that Abraham did not tell her because she would have raised an outcry and would have tried to stop him from carrying out God's instructions, Syriac ones portray Sarah in a much more favourable light, taking their cue (as often) from Ephrem. Ephrem only has a short section on the chapter in his Commentary on Genesis, but what he says proved very influential and has left its mark on both the dialogue and the narrative poem translated here:

He did not reveal it to Sarah since he had not been ordered to reveal it; but had he done so, she would have been beseeching him that she might go and share in his sacrifice, just as he had made her share in the promise of his birth.

The two Syriac poems go a step further than Ephrem in that they portray Sarah as indeed aware of what is to happen; in the dialogue poem she at first upbraids her husband, but then allows him to take Isaac off, having made Abraham swear by God that he would not come to any harm. Since Abraham gives her God as a pledge, implicitly she too is being portrayed as sharing in his complete faith in God's word.

The unknown author of the narrative poem, who clearly knows the dialogue, goes much further, and presents Sarah's faith as even greater than Abraham's, since she has to undergo two trials, instead of his one. At the outset she is well aware of God's command, and she even instructs Isaac how he is to act when his father puts him on the sacrificial pyre. More extraordinary still is the homecoming scene, when Abraham goes in first all alone "to spy out her mind," and she is left to assume that Isaac has indeed been sacrificed. It is only after her moving lament that Isaac finally enters and falls into his mother's arms. Of all the many treatments of the theme in Late Antiquity, this must be one of the boldest and most innovative.

There are two details which are largely confined to the Syriac exegetical tradition to which reference is made in the first of the two poems, and so require brief explanation here. In the Syriac version of Genesis 22.12 the voice from heaven states "Now I have made known . . . ," instead of "Now I know . . . ." This is in fact already found in the Book of Jubilees from the third or second century BC, where the whole episode is seen as being initiated by Mastema (Satan), as in the opening of Job. Syriac authors were not aware of Jubilees' scenario, but they (and the Rabbis) retained the understanding that God was making known Abraham's faith to the angels who did not believe it would hold out under such extreme duress. This is specifically alluded to in stanza 38 of the dialogue.

A little later in the dialogue, in stanza 42, God tells Abraham to "look at the tree that was not planted; it has produced a fruit that was not conceived." The reference is to the ram caught in the thicket (Gen 22.13), but the miraculous origin of the tree and the fruit allude to a tradition that is first found in Ephrem's Commentary:

> That the ram had not been there before is testified by Isaac's question concerning the lamb; and that the tree had not been there before is assured by the wood on Isaac's shoulders. The mountain burst forth with the tree, and the tree with the ram, so that, through the ram that was suspended on the tree and became the sacrifice instead of Abraham's son, that day of his (John 8.56) might be depicted when he was suspended on the wood like the ram and tasted death on behalf of the whole world.

Though Ephrem does not use this as a type of Mary's miraculous birth of Jesus, the dialogue poem obliquely points to it in stanzas 42 and 44; a much more explicit reference will be met with in Ch. IV, no. 4 (Mary and Joseph), stanza 14. In later liturgical poetry one of the many titles given to Mary is "the Tree," based on this passage.

The dialogue poem is, in fact, full of typological parallels between Isaac and Christ. Besides the one just mentioned, we find:

> Abraham and Isaac:: the Father and his Word (stanzas 1, 49);
> barren Sarah's birth of Isaac:: the virgin Mary's birth of Christ (stanza 44);
> Isaac carries the wood:: Christ carries the cross (stanzas 53–4);
> the two young men:: the two thieves crucified with Christ (stanzas 10, 45);
> Isaac "dies," though alive:: Christ dies, though alive (stanza 44);

the sacrifice of Isaac:: the sacrifice of Christ (stanza 55);
the three days' journey: Christ's three days in Sheol (stanza 34);
Sarah's being comforted at Isaac's return: Mary's being comforted at Christ's resurrection (stanza 34);
the pyre: the Holy Table (stanza 49).

What is remarkable about this list is the absence of any typological role given to the ram (apart from the oblique reference implied by stanzas 42 and 44). This contrasts with two other typological patterns to be found in early Christian literature: (1) the lamb/ram is a type for Christ (who is slain), whereas Isaac is a type for humanity (which is rescued); and (2) Isaac is a type for Christ's divinity, untouched by death, whereas the lamb/ram is a type for his humanity, which suffers death.

Although the dialogue poem introduces all these different typological parallels, the narrative poem is very sparing in Christian references. This second poem has quite a number of unusual features, quite apart from the prominent role given to Sarah. The reference to the miraculous fleece which Abraham and Isaac bring back seems to be unique, though one wonders if, at the back of the poet's mind, there was the Greek legend of the Golden Fleece. Behind the reference to fire descending on the sacrifice of Abraham (in line 169) is the idea that the descent of fire from heaven denotes the acceptance of a sacrifice: this is a motif which has already been met in no. 4 of this Chapter, on Abel and Cain.

Translation

1. O Father who asked Abraham for the sacrifice,
    grant me that I may tell the tale
    of Abraham and Isaac who marked out between them
    a type of the Father and the Son.   cf. Rom 8.32

2. O Being who marked out his image in Isaac
    who sprung forth after a hundred years,   Gen 21.5
    grant me utterance without fear
    so that I may tell of the wonder that your might performed.

3. The Father spoke, "Abraham, listen;   Gen 22.1–2
    take Isaac whom you love,
    and offer up to me, as a perfect sacrifice,
    your only-begotten, without being grieved."

4. The upright Abraham was fervent in love
    while faith resided in his heart.   cf. Heb 11.17
    He began to prepare what was required
    for the sacrifice of his son, just as he had been bidden.

5. SARAH: Sarah says, "What are you doing,
    splitting that wood which you have in your hands?
    Might it be that you are going to sacrifice our son
    with that knife that you are sharpening?"

6. ABRAHAM: Abraham says, "Sarah, be silent:
    you are already upset, and you are vexing me.
    This is a hidden mystery,
    which those who love men cannot perceive."

7. SARAH: You are not aware of how much I endured—
    the pains and birth pangs that accompanied his birth.
    Swear to me on him that he will not come to any harm,
    since he is my hope. Then take him, and go.

8. ABRAHAM: The Mighty God in whom I believe
    will act as a pledge to you for me, if you will believe it,
    that Isaac your son will quickly return,
    and you will be comforted by his youthfulness.

9. Abraham left the tent,   Gen 22.3
   and Isaac mounted upon a donkey,
   a type of the Son who rode the colt
   as he entered Jerusalem.   Mt 21.7 and par.

10. Abraham and Isaac travelled on the journey,
    taking with them two young men,   Gen 22.3
    just as Christ went up to the mountain,
    taking with him two stripped men.

11. ABRAHAM (to God): You swore by yourself
    that Isaac's seed would be too numerous to count,

                                              Gen 15.5, 17.2

    but if he is to die, then the agreement
    you made with me will prove false.

12. Your hand has indicated, and your mouth has asked
    that Isaac should be a sacrifice to you;
    by means of the Will, by which he was fashioned,
    show me the mountain where he is to be sacrificed.

13. Abraham raised his eyes upon high   Gen22.4
    and prayed in supplication before the Lord:
    "You, Lord, gave him to me, and now he is required by you;
    show me the place where I should sacrifice him."

14. They travelled on, and when they reached where they started
        climbing
    they left the young men at the foothills.   Gen 22.5
    The Spirit began to sing within them,
    "Blessed is the mystery which is being depicted in us!"

15. ISAAC: Isaac says, "The wood is upon me,
    the fire is with us, but there is no lamb   Gen 22.7

or any pyre built here,
so how can you offer up a sacrifice?"

16. ABRAHAM: Abraham says, "There is the Lord   Gen 22.8
    who will provide the whole offering and the lamb,
    and you will see it hanging by its horns   cf. Gen 22.13
    on a branch, without its having been conceived."

17. ISAAC: Why are you gazing at me and at heaven
    and placing your hand on the knife
    when the lamb that is to be sacrificed
    has not come with us? Why are you making such haste?

18. ABRAHAM: My son, we have not yet reached
    the place where the sacrifice is to be made:
    we still have a little more of the mountain before us,
    and then, once we have arrived, we will have rest.

19. ISAAC: Show me and explain, if it is possible,
    why you did not reveal to Sarah my mother
    the secret between you and the Lord,
    and why did you not take with us a lamb?

20. ABRAHAM: The Hidden One, who called me, will come
          hither
    to see to the lamb he requires:
    you shall see one that has not been conceived
    or been received as fruit in a womb.

21. ISAAC: You seem to me to have heard some voice,
    similar to the one in the tent,   Gen 18.9–10
    the time when you slaughtered a calf from the herd   Gen 18.7
    for the travellers who blessed you—and I was born to you.

22. ABRAHAM: The journey resembles in type
    him who stayed with me as the travellers
    and ate food at our table: Gen 18.8
    he received a calf—and gave you to me.

23. ISAAC: This is hard for me to believe you,
    for I have not heard of a sacrifice without blood
    that was offered by anyone who received an answer
    in the way that you are carrying out just now.

24. ABRAHAM: In this matter which is so hard for you
    is a wondrous portent at which both angels and humanity
    will be amazed, and its report will go forth
    to the generations after us.

25. ISAAC: If a miracle is being accomplished,
    one at which angels and humanity will be amazed,
    what wrong did my aged mother do to you,
    seeing that you did not tell her what you were going to do?

26. ABRAHAM: In return for my not having revealed to her
    the secret between me and the Lord,
    once she has rejoiced to see you back
    I will relate before her, and she will be astonished.

27. ISAAC: Righteous is the Lord to whom Sarah's compassion
    has entrusted me, and I have come here:
    he will turn her sorrow to joy,
    he will free her from grief.

28. ABRAHAM: At the time of your conception the angels who,
        as travellers,
    gave news of your birth, enjoyed the calf;
    and at your resurrection they will have joy
    in the lamb which is born without being conceived.

29. ISAAC: Abraham, you look as if you're unsheathing
    a murderous knife against me;
    consider the pledge you gave to my mother
    whose eyes gaze out for me at every moment.

30. ABRAHAM: As he who brought me out of paganism
    cf. Gen 11.31, Josh 24.2
    wherein I was raised lives on high,
    what I swore to Sarah will not prove false,
    telling her, "your son will return at once."

31. ISAAC: The mountain is barren, the region fearsome;
    the fire and the wood are all ready,
    but where is the whole offering and the lamb for the altar,
    so that I can believe you?

32. ABRAHAM: The mountain is deserted and utterly desolate;
    no man's voice is here to be heard.
    The angels from on high will come down
    astonished at the wonder they behold.

33. ISAAC: For three days now Sarah has been sitting
    in grief, looking out for us.
    Offer up the sacrifice, as you have been bidden.
    Why are you doing nothing, just gazing at me?

34. ABRAHAM: Three days shall the Son be   Mt 12.40
    in the heart of the earth, with those who sleep.
    Like Sarah shall Mary his mother
    be comforted at his resurrection.

35. ISAAC: Gather stones, bring them and build
    a pyre for the sacrifice, like a priest,
    for the mystery hints to me that it is me you will sacrifice;
    but I grieve not at this, for in me you will grow great.

36. Abraham gathered stones and laid them out;
    he applied the fire, and bound his son—
    but a voice cried out to him, "Kill him not,   Gen 22.12
    see how I have become his pledge."

37. ABRAHAM (to God): My son is not more dear to me than
        your command,
    that I should now let him live; you know this.
    Look at his bonds, examine my mind
    to see how ready I am to sacrifice him to you.

38. GOD: It is not that I have not accepted your offering:
    you have revealed to both angels and humanity your love,
                                Gen 22.12 (Syriac)
    so that the ranks on high, and humanity on earth,
    now know that it is me you love.

39. ABRAHAM: Lord, turn not your face from me:
    look at the whole offering already alight.
    If I descend without having made the sacrifice
    I shall be an object of reproach to the world.

40. GOD: The death of your son is quite impotent
    to deliver the Peoples from the curse:
    my Son shall come down, and he will be sacrificed
    in the body he will put on from the womb.

41. ABRAHAM: May my stumbling actions make supplication to
        you not to deprive
    the pyre I have built of its sacrifice.
    And look at Isaac, how sorrowful his tears,
    how he was all expectant to be sacrificed.

42. GOD: You shall slaughter a lamb, and then descend.

Gen 22.13

   Do not suppose that I have not accepted:
   look at the tree that was not planted,
   it has produced a fruit that was not conceived.

43. ABRAHAM: After a hundred years Isaac was the bunch of
      grapes
   which your providence hung upon a barren vine,
   and here he is before you, bound on the pyre:
   I will sacrifice him to you if you so command.

44. The barren Sarah gave birth to a son
   who dies, though alive, being wrapped in a symbol.
   Mary the virgin gave birth to a Son
   who dies though alive, being wrapped in glory.

45. Along with Abraham's son there went up
   to the mountain foothills those two men,
   and in the case of Mary's Son, when he was crucified,
   two robbers accompanied him.

46. The Peoples were astonished at Abraham and Isaac
   who, though bound, was perfect and still.
   The voice which had ordered his death brought him back to
      life
   so that he might become a father to many peoples.

Gen 17.4–5

47. Isaac was bound, and the voice released him—
   that pledge which delivered him—
   so that in him the peoples might receive blessing,   Gen 22.18
   while he was preserved as a symbol for his Lord.

48. Our Lord's body which was wrapped   Mt 27.59
    in clean and scented garments
    went up from Sheol without corruption,
    and the Church received comfort on seeing him.

49. Abraham and Isaac his son were depicted
    as a type of the Father and his Word,
    and for the Church, the pyre became
    the Holy Table, full of Life.

50. The Son's cross became a bridge
    to the place of Life whereby the Peoples
    who have believed and do believe might cross over,
    since it was on our behalf that he tasted death.   Heb 2.9

51. Isaac was slain from the moment that Abraham heard
    the voice which said, "Kill your son";
    but the Lord saved him from having to die,
    thus comforting Sarah who was revived by him.

52. Our Lord was slain through the ill-will
    of Jews, and then was crucified;
    his death razed Jerusalem
    and built up the Church which had faith in him.

53. Great is the mystery, and utterly glorious,
    which Abraham's son performed on the mountain:
    he carried the wood with which to be burnt,
    he went out to die, unaware.

54. A great act of discernment, and much to be wondered at,
    did the Son of God perform on earth:
    he carried the wood on which he was to be crucified,
    and he went forth to die, to deliver all.

55. Praise to the voice which called out to Abraham,
    "Restrain your hand; do not kill
    Isaac, who is sacrificed, though not killed,
    for in that sacrifice is his Lord depicted."

56. Praise to the Son who cried out to his Father,
    "Into your hands do I commend my soul."   Lk 23.46
    Having conquered death and overthrown Sheol
    he has ascended in glory on high.

57. Let Sarah and Isaac her son thank you,
    O Son of the Living One, for he was delivered in you;
    and let upright Abraham, who marked out your type,
    give praise to you, seeing that he grew great and revealed
        your mystery.

58. Let the Church and all her children give thanks
    for the new and immortal life,
    and may those who have received your Body and Blood
    be delivered from Gehenna.

59. O Lord, who dwell above on high,
    who see the depths but are not seen,
    may your peace reign over the world.
    O Christ, who have saved us, to you be all praises!

7. Abraham and Isaac (Genesis 22): anonymous narrative poem

Introduction (see on 6)

Translation

Give me your attention, O hearers,	
to this my fine narrative:	
I begin to lay down before you	
the story of holy people.	
Abraham, father of nations,	5
for a hundred years as though a single day,	Gen 21.5
stood at God's gate	
asking, amid groans	
and with supplication and prayer,	
that he should have a son by Sarah.	10
When he had completed a hundred years	
he began to say as follows,	
"I will stand here another hundred years,	
I will not depart unless I receive a son."	
And our Lord, who saw his wish,	15
straightway sent an angel;	Gen 18.2, 10
he blessed him and increased his possessions,	
and he had a son in his old age.	Gen 21.2
The son was strong and grew up,	
and in him Abraham greatly rejoiced.	20
God called out to Abraham	
and spoke with him and said,	
"Offer up to me your son as a whole offering	Gen 22.2
on one of the mountains I shall tell you of."	
Abraham heard his word	25
and brought a knife and sharpened it.	
Sarah saw and her heart groaned,	
and she began to speak to Abraham,	

"Why are you sharpening your knife?
What do you intend to slaughter with it? 30
This secret today–
why have you hidden it from me?"
And Abraham answered and said
in reply to her words,
"This secret today 35
women cannot be aware of."
Sarah gave answer to Abram
with a groan and great feeling,
"When you brought in the poor
and gave me joy when I was downcast 40
—for even the poor whom we received
turned out to be angels— Gen 18
they can testify to my mind,
if what you had in mind was not the same as I had.
You are drunk with the love of God, 45
who is the God of gods,
and if he so bids you concerning the child
you will kill him without hesitation:
let me go up with you to the burnt offering,
and let me see my only child being sacrificed; 50
if you are going to bury him in the ground
I will dig the hole with my own hands,
and if you are going to build up stones,
I will carry them on my shoulders;
the lock of my white hairs in old age 55
will I provide for his bonds.
But if I cannot go up
to see my only child being sacrificed
I will remain at the foot of the mountain
until you have sacrificed him and come back." 60
Sarah took her only child
and began to speak to him as follows,

words full of wonder,
and with a groan she said,
"When you go with your father,   65
listen and do all that he tells you,
and if he should actually bind you,
stretch out your hands to the bonds;
and if he should actually sacrifice you,
stretch out your neck before his knife: 70
stretch out your neck like a lamb,
like a kid before the shearer.   Is 53.7
See, my son, that you do not put your father under oath
when he draws out his knife against you,
lest his mind be upset   75
and there be a blemish in his offering.
And listen, my son, to the words of your mother,
and let your reputation go forth unto generations to come."
She embraced him and kissed him amid tears,
and said to him, "Go in peace;   80
may the God who gave you to me
return you to me in safety."
She took Isaac by the right hand
and handed him over to the upright Abram.
Abraham led off his son;   85
he set out and made for the mountains.
They travelled for a day and a second,
and the whole of the third,   Gen 22.4
when a voice came from on high,
"This is the mountain of which I spoke to you;   90
take down the wood from the donkey,
and load it onto the child.   Gen 22.6
Behold, I shall put in him strength
so that he can take it up to the mountain top,
and in this way I too shall carry   95
my cross in the streets of Sion,   Jn 19.17

and when I go down to Golgotha
I will effect the salvation of Adam."
The child began to speak,
saying as follows, 100
"My father, whither have you led me, and I have come,
with no other person with us?
On the pretext of a sheep you took me, and I came,
but there is no sheep in the wilderness." Gen 22.7
Abraham said to his son, 105
the blessed old man to his only-begotten,
"God will see to a lamb Gen 22.8
for the burnt offering which he himself has wanted."
Abraham began to build Gen 22.9
for his mind was prepared, 110
while Isaac brought along stones
on his shoulders to Abraham.
They became workers for God,
the old man and his son, equally,
and beautiful were their labors, 115
and their actions equal.
The Threefold One blessed them
for they had become workers for his Being.
The building of the pyre was completed,
and the affair came out into the open. 120
The child began to adjure,
saying as follows,
"My father, <what is this?>
The pyre is built and completed;
where is the lamb, as you said, Gen 22.7 125
for here on the mountain there are no sheep?"
Abraham showed him the bonds,
and Isaac folded his hands:
"I know, my father, that it is coming to me
to be the lamb for the whole offering; 130

draw near, father, and bind me,
tie tightly for me my bonds,
lest my limbs should shake,
and there be a blemish in your sacrifice.
Sarah was wanting to see me   135
when I was bound like a lamb,
and she would have wept beside me with lamentation,
and by her tears I would have received comfort.
O my mother Sarah, I wish
I could see you, and then be sacrificed."   140
Abraham greatly rejoiced
at what he heard from the child,
for he imagined in his mind
that he would be offering up supplication
<with cries of grief to God>   145
to deliver him from the knife.
So Abraham bound his son,   Gen22.9
and carried him and placed him on the pyre;
he raised his eyes up to heaven
and cried, "Bless, O Lord."   150
He stretched out his hand for the knife   Gen 22.10
<and it reached his dear son's neck>
when all of a sudden the heaven was opened,
and the Lord's right hand overshadowed
as a voice came from on high,   Gen 22.11 155
"Abraham, hold back from the child;
your offering is accepted from this moment,
your discernment is accepted likewise,
and the child shall return in safety
and become father to thousands without number;
            Gen 22.17 160
and without mention of your name, Abraham,
an offering will not be accepted.
Look, a lamb is hanging on the tree;

take the lamb and offer it up in his place."
Abraham ran to the tree   Gen 22.13   165
and brought down from it the lamb;
he sacrificed it and offered it up as a whole offering
<in place of Isaac his beloved son>.
And fire came down from on high,
and accepted the offering of Abram.   170
Abraham and Isaac sat down
and ate the flesh of the burnt offering,
while the Lord was pleased with the offering
of Abram the upright and just.
Abraham led away his son,   175
and they set off and came down the mountain.
The child carried the fleece
which had, in a mystery, delivered him on the mountain.
The young men saw the fleece that had come,
and they gave thanks in return.   180
For what might be the telling of this fleece
which does not resemble the fleece of ordinary sheep:
its appearance is of all sorts of colours,
and there is no comparison to its form.
But for the eye of the prophets,   185
it would not be possible to examine it.
Once he had arrived and reached home
Abraham said to his son,
"O my son, please stay back for a little:
I will go in and return to your mother,   190
and I will see how she receives me;
I will spy out her mind and her thought."
The old man returned and entered in peace:
Sarah rose up to receive him;
she brought him a bowl to wash his feet,   195
and she began to say as follows,
"Welcome, blessed old man,

husband who has loved God;
welcome, O happy one,
who has sacrificed my only child on the pyre;   200
welcome, O slaughterer,
who did not spare the body of my only child.
Did he weep when he was bound,
or groan as he died?
He was greatly looking out for me,   205
but I was not there to come to his side;
his eyes were wandering over the mountains,
but I was not there to deliver him.
By the God whom you worship,
relate to me the whole affair."   210
Abraham answered and said
to Sarah in reply to her words,
"Your son did not weep when he was bound,
he gave no groan when he died.
You have put me under an oath by God   215
saying "Did he ask to see you on the pyre?"
When the pyre was built and set up,
and the bonds were over his hands
and the knife above his neck,
then did he remember you there,   220
and he asked to see you on the pyre."
<Then Sarah said in response,>
"May the soul of my only child be accepted,
for he hearkened to the words of his mother.
I wish I were an eagle,   225
or had the speed of a turtle-dove,
so that I might go and behold that place
where my only child, my beloved, was sacrificed,
that I might see the place of his ashes,
and look on the place of his binding,   230
and bring back a little of his blood

to be comforted by its smell.
I had some of his hair
to place somewhere inside my clothes,
and when grief overcame me   235
I placed it over my eyes.
I had some of his clothes,
so that I might imagine him, as I put them in front of my eyes;
and when suffering sorrow overcame me
I gained relief through gazing upon them.   240
I wish I could see his pyre
and the place where his bones were burnt,
and could bring a little of his ashes,
and gaze on them always, and be comforted."
And as she stood, her heart mourning,   245
her mind and thought intent,
greatly upset with emotion,
her mind dazed as she grieved,
the child entered, having come back safe and sound.
Sarah arose to receive him,   250
she embraced him and kissed him amidst tears,
and began to address him as follows,
"Welcome, my son, my beloved,
welcome, child of my vows;
welcome, O dead one come to life,   255
<welcome, O child who has come back from the grave.">
The child then began to speak,
saying as follows,
"A son does not last forever,
nor do wealth and possessions,   260
but God endures for ever
for him who performs his will.
But for the voice which called out
"Abraham, hold off from the child"   Gen 22.11–12
I would yesterday have died,   265

and my bones would have been consumed by fire."
Then Sarah began to repay,
with utterances of thanksgiving,
the Good One who had returned her only child
<in safety from the mountain>,   270
"I give thanks to God
who has given you to me a second time;
I worship that Voice
which delivered you, my son, from the knife.
I praise him who has saved you   275
from burning on the pyre.
Henceforth, my son, it will not be "Sarah's son"
that people will call you,
but "child of the pyre,"
and "offering which died and was resurrected."   280
And to you be glory, O God,
for all passes away, but you endure."

8. Tamar and Judah (Genesis 38): Jacob of Serugh, verse homily

Introduction

The biblical text of Genesis 38 describes how Tamar's first two
husbands, both sons of Judah, died without providing her with any
children (verses 6–10). Judah promises her that she should be given
in marriage to his next son, Shelah, when he grew up (verse 11), but
when he does, the promise is not kept (verse 14). It is at this point
that in her desperation Tamar resorts to an unconventional ruse
in order to have offspring from Judah's family: she dresses up as a
prostitute and seduces her father-in-law, Judah (verses 14–16). This
was an action for which, according to Leviticus 20.12, they should
both have been put to death, yet the biblical narrator leaves them
without any word of reproach. As Jacob suggests in the extended

preliminary invocation to this striking verse homily, there must be some reason why the episode was included in the sacred text. For both Jewish and early Christian exegetes, the key to a proper, and deeper, understanding of the passage lies in God's promise to Abraham that all the peoples of the earth would be blessed in "his seed" (Gen 22.18), who is identified as the Messiah (thus, explicitly, Paul in Galatians 3.16). Accordingly the gentile Tamar is included in the Davidic line in 1 Chronicles 2.4 and in the genealogy of Christ in Matthew 1.3. Tamar's action was thus seen as being motivated by a desire to become an ancestor of the Messiah. In his Commentary on Genesis Ephrem has Tamar say, "It is for what is hidden in the Hebrews that I thirst," and on another occasion he wrote:

> See, the King was hidden in Judah: Tamar stole him from
> his loins.
> Today there has shone out the splendour of the beauty
> whose hidden form she loved!
>
> (Hymns on the Nativity 1:12)

In a similar vein, on the Jewish side, the late Midrash ha-Gadhol states that "The Spirit of Holiness said, 'Neither has Tamar incited fornication, nor has Judah sought to fornicate: it is from me that the matter originates, since the King Messiah will arise from Judah.'"

In the opening line Jacob puns on her name, for in Syriac the opening two words are *Ta Mar(y)*, "Come, Lord," which in turn alludes to Paul's quotation of the Aramaic phrase *Marana ta*, "our Lord, come!" in 1 Corinthians 16.22. As is often the case, Jacob is simply picking up a hint already provided by Ephrem (Hymns on the Nativity 9.12).

Translation

Come, Lord, to me, and bring the mercy of your kindness;
sprinkle it on my strings, and let them extol you with their songs.
Come, my Lord and my God, and blow in me as into an empty
    reed
so that I may give forth sounds with a stirring of love, without
    confusion.
Come, O Lord, and grant me fair utterance that is filled with
    beauty   5
so that I may speak thereby, as I worship in great wonder.
Come, you who are not distant in giving each day all kinds of
    good things
to the person who seeks to receive freely the wealth that comes
    from you.
You are close by, O Son of God, you are close at hand
to grant each day all kinds of requests for those who ask.   10
You are close by, and here you are, with us, Emmanuel:
you have wearied yourself by bringing blessings and riches for
    the entire world.
You were with us, and like us too, all for our sakes,
and now heights and depths worship you in their domains.
The height sent you, and the depth received you in great
    wonder,   15
and look, height and depth are filled by you, for you are
    boundless.
You came to the world–and the heights were not emptied of you,
you resided in the Virgin–and the heaven remained full of your
    glory.
All the heights, in their domains, are not sufficient for you,
and see how all the depths, and those who dwell in them hold
    you in honour.   20
You came from the Father; you shone out from a mother;
    you became an infant.

Mercy mingled you with humanity, so that you might save it.
You scattered your treasures over the poor and made them rich,
the dead came to life in you, and the world, that had become
    corrupted, was set in order.
You became the Daytime, and the whole earth became light
    from you: 25
night fled away, for all creation had been submerged in it.
You came down like rain upon the lands that lay waste;
you made them like Paradise full of blessings.
You shone out as the Sun of righteousness over the entire earth,

                                         Mal 4.2

and your Dawn dissipated the darkness from every region.   30
You are the Bread of Life, for the dead consumed you and were
    resurrected in you.   Jn 6.35, 48
You are the good wine, for by you all who mourn are comforted.
With oil, you consigned to oblivion the wickedness of Adam who
    had been smitten;
you applied wine to his wounds, seeing that he had been
    wounded;   Lk 10.34
with living water you cleansed away his filth, for he had become
    sullied,   35
and he was renewed in you, and returned to Eden which he had
    lost.
O Son of God, exalted in your highway and full of blessings,
set out upon it are the milestones of peace for him who travels on
    it.
You, Lord, are the Light; you are Life, Lord; you are the
    Resurrection.   Jn 11.25
You are the great Treasure Store by whose treasures the
    poor have become rich.   40
When your compassionate Father fashioned Adam in
    his image   Gen 1.26–7
it was you he depicted in him, for in you the dust that had
    multiplied would be adorned.

He gave to Adam your likeness when he created him, so that he
    might put it on
and by it reign over all created things and acquire them.
With a breath of life did Christ make him when
    he made him,   Gen 2.7   45
so that he might keep his place in the world until he would
    come.
You were hidden in your Father, and he revealed you in Adam
    when he created him:
he depicted in him the likeness of your bodily existence and your
    revelation.
The depiction of the King travelled down all the generations,
transmitted mysteriously over the lineages,   50
so that God himself might be mingled amongst humanity.
He gave his image from the very beginning of Creation so that
    human beings might be made in it,
for he was preparing to send his Son, the Only-Begotten;
and in this same fashion he came into the open, in bodily form:
for in the likeness of the Only-Begotten of the Godhead   55
he depicted Adam when he fashioned him, in a great mystery.
He (then) came back and took the likeness of his servant from
    within the womb,   cf. Phil 2.7
and became like him while he was delivering him from the
    Rebel.
He came to his nativity, he took up his likeness, he delivered his
    image.
He commenced and he completed in accordance with
    his will in great love.   60
The upright throughout the generations held his likeness in
    honour,
and for this reason the remembrance of them became
    resplendent.
The fair Seth, who resembles his father, delineated
    him,   Gen 4.25

so that the world might see that the Son of God resembled him.
Noah the just in that Ark which performed mysteries   65
depicted an image for him, in that he was rescued from the
     Flood.
To Abraham the Father spoke in
     revelation,   Gen 22.18, Gal 3.16
saying that all the peoples would be blessed in his elect seed.
And because of this the Son of God was expected,
for the world had become aware that he would come in a
     mysterious way.   70
All the upright were desirous to see his day   Mt 13.17
and were expecting he would shine forth on earth in their own
     days.
In various places women were yearning for the choice seed—
that from them he who was expected to come to earth might
     shine forth:
Leah and Rachel, straightforward women of integrity,   75
were contending over him in the land of Aram.
They had heard that in the seed of the House of Abraham
all the peoples were going to be blessed–and fire fell upon their
     minds!
For this reason there befell a dispute between the two of them,
and, as if over some treasure, they fought over a
     righteous man.   80
They performed an action that was most hateful to chaste
     women:
one desired, and one asked, impudently;
they acted without restraint, showing no shame, because they
     were aware
of what wealth was concealed in the godly man.
Rachel, importunate and like a prostitute, demanded
     of him,   85
saying, "Give me children, otherwise I will die."   Gen 30.1

Leah, like someone infatuated and loving adultery,
    hired him,   Gen 30.16
and she was not ashamed to plunder the wealth that she so
    desired.
It was not with the lust of adulterous women that they were fired,
but it was for the seed of their weighty man that they longed.   90
Ruth too acted in like fashion over Boaz,   Ruth 3
going out in the night like a thief to despoil
so that she might steal from him the great wealth that was hidden
    within him.
She was not ashamed, chaste woman that she was,
    to seize hold of his legs.   Ruth 3.7–8
She went out to the threshing floor to steal away the seed of the
    House of Abraham.   Ruth 3.6   95
In her vigilance she stole it, just as she had wanted, in an
    impudent way.
When and how have women so run after men
as these women who contended over the Medicine of Life?
The divine plan, mistress of mysteries, incited these women
with love of the Only-Begotten before he had ever come.   100
It was because of him that they acted without restraint and
    schemed,
putting on the outward guise of wanton women,
despising female modesty and nobility,
not being ashamed as they panted for men.
Someone who wants to get hold of a treasure, if he could,   105
would perform a murder in order to gain the gold he so desired.
These women, while running after men,
were yearning for the Son of God's great Epiphany,
and they struggled for the seed of the House of Abraham,
since they had learnt that in it the Peoples of the earth
    would be blessed.   110
It was not harlotry in the case of these sincere women,
but love for the blessed seed that incited them.

As though it were gold, and as though it were great riches,
they seized the fair seed from the farmers of renown.
Like a prostitute or flighty woman, Ruth went out   115
to the aged Boaz, without his being aware, but she remained
     chaste.
It was a desire filled with faith that stirred the aged man
to take a wife at an unexpected time,   Ruth 4.10
and (so) the faith of her who had sought him was not
     disappointed,
and just as she had asked, the pearl was granted to her,   120
and she conceived and gave birth to the father of Jesse, the man
     from Ephratha;   Ruth 4.17
and it was from him that David, the godly king, sprouted forth.
So, in the case of Leah who had hired Jacob,
the great wealth for which she had yearned was thus acquired for
     her.
But what should I say concerning Tamar, who is filled with
     mysteries?   125
For the wonder that fills her case surpasses that of her
     companions:
this woman openly became a wanton-hearted prostitute,
she went out and sat by the crossroads to ensnare a man!
It was for you, O Son of God, that she was gazing out, waiting for
     you to come to her,
and it was because of you that she despised women's
     nobility.   130
She went out after you like an infatuated woman in the streets,
for she was wanting you to sprinkle sanctity on her limbs.
Now Tamar saw that if she sat like an honourable woman
she would not ensnare the wealth after which she had gone out.
Therefore she dressed like a prostitute, went out and sat
     there,   135
to fall in with a merchant on the road, like some wanton-hearted
     woman.

In the case of all the mystery-filled narratives of the Only-
     Begotten
it is right to listen with great love, O discerning reader,
for if love does not open the gate of your ear
then there is no passage to your hearing for the words.   140
In the case of the story of Tamar, unless a mind that has faith
listens to it, the discerning woman will seem worthy of reproach,
whereas if an intellect that loves to listen to the mysteries
should hear this tale, it will render back in return for it praise.
All the words that the Spirit of God has placed in Scripture   145
are filled with riches, like treasures, hidden in the different books.
Moses the scribe set the story of Tamar   Gen 38
like a jewel in his Book so that its beauty might shine out
     amongst its lections.
Why would he have written of a woman who sat like a
     prostitute   Gen 38.14–15
by the crossroads had she not been filled with some
     mystery?   150
Why did Moses, who drove away all prostitutes from his
     people,   cf. Deut 23.17–18, Num 25
extol this one who had adorned herself like a prostitute?
Her action would have been wrong had there not been some
     mystery there,
and it would not have been successful had it been something
     hateful to God.
Her action was indeed ugly, but her faith made it
     beautiful,   155
and it was resplendent and dear because of the Mystery that was
     performed in her.
Moses, who was the mediator of the Law
laid reproof and a curse on the man who was the cause of
     fornication,
whereas in the case of Judah he did not reprove or lay a curse on
     him,   cf. Lev 20.12

nor did he reproach him, for he knew that there was some
    mystery there.   160
Maybe you will say that he was not aware that she was his
    daughter-in-law,
but then I will say to you, he knew very well that she was a
    prostitute,
and yet Moses did not reproach him saying, Why did he go to a
    prostitute?
Instead, he put him there amongst the readings, without
    reproving him.
Tamar's faith was beautiful to God,   165
and this is what set aright an ugly affair that would otherwise
    have been corrupt.
For had her faith not been filled with mysteries,
Moses would not have reserved a portrait of beauty for a woman
    who played the prostitute;
nor would Judah have escaped from blame,
seeing that his path to the prostitute resembled that of a
    debauched man.   170
When Jacob his father was dying, he wrote as follows
in his Testament, that all his brothers should laud him,

                Gen 49.8

and Moses blessed him, and no mention was made of any lapse.
Both Moses and Jacob described him as an upright man.
We should accordingly say that even though he committed
    fornication,   175
the divine economy compelled him, out of love for the faith.
Tamar's prayer, together with her faith, bent down
the exalted mystery so that it bent itself down to great dishonour.
Therefore listen now in a discerning way concerning Tamar,
look at the radiant woman, filled with all the beauty of faith. 180
This woman entered Judah's household and became a daughter-
    in-law,   Gen 38.6
while faith in the house of Abraham was burning within her.

She took pride in the blessed seed of the great race
and held in expectation that from her the Messiah would shine
    forth when he came.
While she was fired with faith, her husband died.

Gen 38.7   185

She trembled and felt diminished: her heart was shattered,
    deprived of her expectation.
His brother—a cunning man—took her, although he did not
    want to,   Gen 38.8–10
not thinking of the good, he disappointed her of the seed,
    refusing to give it her;
but the upright Lord gave judgement on him and slew him as
    well.
She sat in mourning—a field left without any farmers: 190
the first had died, having sown without any crops,
the second had died, having disappointed the field by failing to
    sow it.
The bride who was filled with exalted beauty and sagacity
was rejected: she buried her husbands, and gave herself to
    thought.
She sat down, setting her gaze on a child from the family of
    Judah,   Gen 38.11   195
whether there might be one, waiting for him in her sagacity.
It was for the clan of the house of Abraham that she was
    yearning,
and she felt under compulsion to wait for a Savior to shine forth
    from her.
But because the family of Judah had rejected this sage woman
    saying,
"Because she has buried two husbands, let her not go on to bury
    a third!"   200
They regarded her as being like a field full of thorns
which smothers the seedlings and fails to provide a crop to every
    farmer.

So they neglected it and abandoned it to become wild ground,
    uncultivated:
there was not a single farmer who was not afraid to approach it.
She was treated unjustly, humiliated, and put to shame;   205
she was pained, broken, and afflicted;
and because the family of Judah had cut her off from them
    entirely
yet the woman was burning with a desire for fruit, what should
    she do?
A ray of light from the hidden mysteries shone forth strongly in
    her soul,
and she set off at a run in the direction of the
    Only-Begotten.   210
Were she to sit down quietly and in modesty stay at home
                          Gen 38.11
they would never think of her and she would be deprived of her
    hope.
In order to urge them to provide a husband to be with her
she holds herself contemptible, while they scorn her and have
    nothing to do with her.
So she felt constrained to begin to seek out how she might
    find a way   215
of stealing the blessed seed, and so be comforted by it.
With an idea that was full of hope and faith
she set a trap to enmesh Judah himself
and so from the very Treasure Store to bring out the treasure that
    is full of riches,
from which there would shine forth great wealth for the entire
    world.   220
So it was from God that she asked in prayer that he would give
    her
the treasure she wanted from the clan of upright men.
She peered out and looked how he came and went
so that she might spread out the snares and the nets in his path.

When she had learnt in what direction his path took him

                                    Gen 38.13   225

she set her face to the action that she intended:

straight away she stripped off chastity and nobility

                                    Gen 38.14

and took to the road in the garb of loose women.

She took off and laid aside the garments of mourning that she
    had been wearing

and, like a prostitute, she put on the clothes of flighty
    women   230

and hurriedly she set out; she sat down and kept her eyes on the
    road

for when that merchant might pass by—to be plundered by her.

The soul, heart and eyes of Tamar, so full of beauty,

were raised up to God as she supplicated him:

while from the outside she was clothed in the garb of loose
    women,   235

within, she was filled with the beauty of holy chastity.

From the exterior, a prostitute, vexed and full of faults,

but within, a soul which was radiant with the future shining forth
    of the Only-Begotten.

Suffering was in her heart, but with merriment shed over her
    face.

She was both praying and laughing: her soul groaned
    out to God,   240

her eyes' gaze intent, on her tongue every kind of request:

she was struggling how she might lay hold of the great crown.

Judah came along; he reached her and was going to pass
    her by,   Gen 38.15–16

but in her faith Tamar stood up and stopped him.

He stood gazing at her, whether he liked it or not;   245

he examined her, how she was both chaste and loose:

she was hiding her face, and was seen only under a veil.

She stole a glance, as though she was not looking, out of her
    modesty;

She incited him to look at her face, to see how fair it was,

but she was covered up, so that he might think that she really was
    modest.   250

So, while she was covered up, he was peering at her beauty
    through her veil

—so that this was a snare in which the "Lion's whelp" would get
    entangled.   Gen 49.9

By means of two kinds of beauty did she contend with the mighty
    man

—with the face's beauty, and with the modesty which he saw in
    her.

Once he had given up his plan to pass by, so as not to associate
    with a prostitute,   255

he stopped to look at her, to see how modest she was; he
    approached her.

She was covered up, so that Judah should not recognise who she
    was,

while he was amazed at her, imagining to himself that this was
    out of modesty.

Now because God's providence was involved

in that affair, Judah was not able to win: 260

Tamar's prayer, and her intention, so full of beauty,

caused the heart of that upright man to turn aside to the
    prostitute.

God saw how much she was longing for the Epiphany of his Son,

and because she was worthy, he granted her to find what she
    wanted.

Her heart rejoiced at intercourse with the upright man,   265

for she had snatched wealth from the merchant, and he then
    passed on.

The Lord granted to her, because he saw her faith,

that she should give birth to two sons, seeing that she had buried
    two husbands.   Gen 38.27

The upright Lord, because he had taken her husbands away from
    her,

granted to her children, and so provided the reward for
    her faith.   270

Tamar was exultant, for she had set a snare and made a catch, as
    she had asked,

and she began to ask for her wages, in insolence, like a
    prostitute: Gen 38.17–18

she took the man's ring and staff, and a scarf too,

three witnesses to be at hand for her at a time of great peril.

He gave them as pledges, not knowing what he was doing: 275

he had been robbed and plundered, yet he provided witnesses so
    that he might be accused!

He gave pledges, as you have heard, and returned to his journey.

The affair was accomplished, faith having brought it about.

The field had received the blessed seed for which it had been
    yearning.

Tamar turned back and entered her house; she took the garments
    of mourning and put them on.   Gen 38.19   280

No one saw what she had done by the crossroads

apart from the Fashioner alone, who fashioned in her the infants.

It was the Lord who kept her secret in that whole affair,

for she did not reveal what she was doing to anyone except him.

Mysteriously, and in a hidden way, he fashioned in her   285

two fair images, causing them to grow in a hidden way for that
    sage woman.

Tamar maintained the mourning for her husbands while she was
    pregnant.

Though she was rejoicing, she was seen to be in mourning:

her heart was exultant at the beloved fruit with which her womb
    was filled.

Like a widow, and one who had lost her children, she was dressed
    in mourning,   290
but she was radiant at the staff, at the ring and at the scarf,
cherishing them like children and heirs.
The secret remained hidden from the farmer, who was unaware
that seed had dropped from him, and the field had caught it up
    from him.
Tamar felt pride, being encouraged and confident   295
that, once the affair had come to light, she would not be
    overcome:
she had three witnesses, carefully guarded, to win her cause.
She was not afraid if she was numbered among adulterous
    women.
Once the blessed seedling had grown and turned into a sheaf,
her belly made it known to people that Tamar was pregnant.
                                   Gen 38.24   300
The woman is modest, her head bowed down, in her mourning
    garb,
yet her womb is with child—so what were people to say about the
    wretched woman?
She sits there in modesty, like a widow full of grief,
but the fact is that she is pregnant: what is one to say? What
    should one ask?
The neighbours will testify to her modesty and noble
    character,   305
her barren and lowly state in which she was sitting,
but Tamar's belly openly testifies to anyone who sees her
that she has seen some man, and all her actions are full of deceit.
Word went out amongst the entire tribe that Tamar was
    pregnant—
a source of grief and great pain to her dear ones and
    friends.   310
Judah's whole household bristled with threats and
    denouncements,

along with numerous insults to the outcast woman.
But Tamar sat there, serene and silent, unperturbed,
for she was confident, feeling no shame over the matter.
Word quickly reached the ear of Judah, and it shattered him:

Gen 38.24   315

he was upset and aggrieved, just man that he was, at the vile deed,
and like an upright judge he was stirred up by what she had done.
He enquired to learn whether it was true that Tamar was
    pregnant;
he then gave sentence, upright man that he was, according to his
    sense of right:
"Take her out to be burnt, in view of the adultery that she has
    despicably committed."   Gen 38.24   320
Look, discerning reader, how resplendent that Hebrew was:
he did not provide an opportunity for foul adultery to be
    performed,
yet he himself was aware of what he had fallen into at the hands
    of Tamar.
Providence had instructed him, because of the strategem:
he was not lax, and did not act as an adulterer or fornicator,   325
but as an upright man who abhors adultery and holds it in check.
And so, when he had learnt that she was pregnant, against the
    Law,   Lev 21.9
he decreed burning by fire for the adulteress, and sent her off to
    be burnt.
He sat there judging her: he sentenced her and handed her over
    to the flame,
just as Moses too was to burn the adulteresses in the fire.

cf. Lev 21.10   330

Even before the Lawgiving, the upright Judah laid down the law
that a woman who is discovered having committed adultery
    should be burnt by fire.
And so this sentence of the upright Judah received its fulfilment.

They rushed off to bring the bereaved woman to the place of
    burning;
they grab her and rebuke her as they tear at her,   335
they drive her off to go to be food for the fire.
While the avengers surrounded Tamar on every side
she dashed off for the pledges, in order to show them—
the ring and the staff, and also the scarf she took up—these
    secrets—
and sent them to the just judge, for him to see.   340
"My lord judge, I have witnesses: summon them and let them
    attend: Gen 38.25
look at them, and if they are genuine, accept them.
Ask the staff and the scarf about the affair;
take a look at the ring, whose seal-stone it is: it will not deceive.
That you are upright and just everyone knows.   345
Investigate the case, look at the witnesses, and then give your
    sentence.
Why should I burn when I have witnesses who will show me to
    be innocent?
Son of Israel, judge a bereaved woman justly."
Judah saw the accusing objects, and realised that they were his;
                             Gen 38.26
the upright man shook, for guilt had suddenly seized him.   350
The staff indicated to him "I am yours: leave off judgement."
The scarf cried out "Hold back the fire from the wretched woman,"
while the ring says, "I am inscribed, and have been kept intact;
my master knows me, and if I get lost, his name will testify for
    me.
Stop the conflagration; remove the fire from this free-born
    woman.   355
Take the pledges, abandon the case, and pronounce innocence."
The just judge saw his own witnesses from inside his own house;
he rushed to remove the condemnation, so that Tamar should
    come out of it innocent.

His anger abated, his fire was quenched, he hung his head,
acknowledging openly that, "She is more innocent than I; let her
    not be abused."   Gen 38.26   360
The conflagration died down, the fire was put out, and Tamar was
    proved innocent.
Like an athlete who had won in the arena, she received a crown.
Well done, Tamar, so full of beauty! I am full of wonder at you.
Your entire story runs its course accompanied by parables and
    types.
Christ the Sun was conveyed over the generations,

                              Mal 4.2   365

and by his Epiphany that will descend from you the entire
    creation will be illumined.
You are a widow, a prostitute, a woman of noble birth all in one,
who acts furtively, but is filled with the beauty of righteousness.
To tell of Tamar's pledges is a source of astonishment,
how they were secretly kept by her in order to rescue her.   370
Whom did she resemble as she was travelling by the crossroads,
what image did she portray there, sage woman that she was?
For it was for the Savior that both the Church and Tamar were
    yearning,
and Tamar trod out the way for the Church, thus instructing her
to seek for the Savior of the Ages by the crossroads,   375
and to take three sureties from the Savior,
once she had found him, then a ring, a staff and also a scarf
she should take from him, and keep with her for they would
    effect her innocence:
faith, Baptism and the cross of light,
the three witnesses which will deliver her from Gehenna.   380
The upright Judah, when he went to see his sheep

                              Gen 38.13

found Tamar by the wayside and he turned aside to her,
and the Son of God, in order to visit the sheep—humankind—

came down from his home, and the Church fell in love with him,
    wanting to be his.
She took as pledges from him, the Savior,   385
faith, Baptism, and the cross of light,
and they are preserved and kept by her intact,
for by them she will overcome the flames of the great judgement,
when the awesome Judge takes his seat on the mighty tribunal,
and all peoples and ages will enter before him for
    judgement.   390
He will give sentence against the wicked and the evil-doers,
exacting judgement on the rebellious by means of fierce flames,
but if he summons the Church, to judge her with the fire,
she will produce and show the three witnesses she has kept safe:
she will show forth the staff—the cross—at which the fire will feel
    shame,   395
and Baptism, which quenches the flame.
Faith is the king's signet ring at which
Judgement's fire feels awe when it is kindled against the
    audacious.
The ring for Tamar, for the Daughter of the Peoples faith
quenches amidst the fire the burning flame;   400
the staff for Tamar, for the Daughter of the Peoples the cross
    stands by
to save her from the flames, so that she is not burnt.
If the scarf, because she had kept it, showed that Tamar was
    innocent,
how much more will the Bride of Light prove innocent?
O Church, persevere, and take care of these three pledges,   405
then they will establish your innocence at the great Judgement.
Preserve with great care faith in the Son of God;
in purity preserve Baptism, full of life.
Take hold of the cross if he summons you to the flames:
show these, and they will rescue from burning.   410
O soul who, like a prostitute, love the world,

supplicate Christ by the wayside, and once you have found him,
take refuge in faith that is filled with light.
Clothe yourself in Baptism, as the armour of righteousness,
and hang the cross of light around your neck, as a
    necklace;   415
then you will have confidence that the flame will not touch you.
Let Tamar serve as a mirror for the entire world:
let everyone preserve his faith and his Baptism,
and when the fire of judgement is revealed in this life,
blessed is he who rescues from the flame the person who loves
    him.   420

9. Joseph and Potiphar's wife (Genesis 39): anonymous dialogue poem

Introduction

The dramatic history of the patriarch Joseph, sold into Egypt by
his brothers and ending up as second only to Pharaoh, caught the
imagination of many early Christian writers. Among the many
texts in Syriac is an entire epic in twelve books, either by Ephrem
himself or by Balai, a poet of the following generation. The episode
where the wife of Potiphar, his master, tried to seduce him (Genesis
39.7–20) lent itself well to the genre of the dialogue poem, and two
such poems exist in Syriac; the older one, which is translated below,
is unfortunately not preserved complete (and in verses 6 and 7 some
lines have been lost); sufficient, however, survives to warrant its
inclusion here. As usual in these dialogue poems there is an alphabetic acrostic: this begins with the fourth stanza, and only reaches
the eighth letter of the Syriac alphabet.

Translation

1. The story of Joseph has come to my mind,
    how he was involved in a mighty dispute,
    but in his ordeal with the woman of Egypt
    the upright man stood unmoved.

2. The woman saw how fair he was:
    his appearance was attractive and handsome.   Gen 39.6
    Burning lust for him broke out in her body
    as she burned with desire for him.

3. She put forth incitements—but he was not won over;
    sweet words of persuasion—but he did not bend.
    She knelt down in reverence and cajoled him,
    but he was not caught up in her nets.

4. WOMAN: The woman says, "Listen, Joseph,
    carry out my desire and sleep with me;   Gen 39.7
    O Hebrew, don't torture me,
    for a burning love for you has flown into my heart."

5. JOSEPH: Joseph says, "Listen, woman,
    calm yourself down from all this;
    even if I'm thirsty, I'm not going to drink
    from stolen water, but only from my own fountain."

                                                          cf. 1 Kg 13.16–22

6. WOMAN: Don't be disturbed about stolen water,
    for no one can see when it is being drunk.

7. JOSEPH: There is the hidden God who cannot be seen,

                                                          cf. Gen 39.9
    but who sees and is well aware when it is being drunk.

8. WOMAN: The waves of my love for you batter my heart,
    and I can't get away from them.
    Listen to me, Joseph, and I'll give you your freedom,
    and you shall have honour in Egypt.

9. JOSEPH: The waves of your lust for me have hoisted you up,
    as if you were a boat, out of all other considerations;
    they have battered at the freedom of your marriage
    and at the companionship of your married life.

10. WOMAN: Maybe I'm not crowned with beauty,
    perhaps I have not put on enough adornments,
    or I've not used the right perfume,
    seeing that you soul shrinks from my desire.

11. JOSEPH: It may be that my master has held back
                                        cf. Gen 39.8–9
    something from me, and not given me authority—
    but in the case of you, who are his wife,
    how could I do such a wicked deed?

12. WOMAN: It is precisely this, Joseph, that I am asking for;
    if it comes to blame,
    have no worries in all this affair,
    for no one else is involved in the secret.

13. JOSEPH: O woman of Egypt, the God
    of Abraham and of Isaac his son,
    and of Jacob my father, who begot me,
    uncovers all secrets and investigates them.

14. WOMAN: Alas for you, Joseph, what has happened to you?
    Won't you listen to what I am saying,
    or bend your ear to my plaint,
    or hear my words and consent to me?

15. JOSEPH: Alas for me, woman, if I should listen to you,
     act as you say and ravish you,
     for even if it were hidden from my master,
     it will not be hidden from God.

16. WOMAN: It is something terrible what you say,
     that, except for this, you are not afraid:
     but as for you, you haven't got any wife,
     so why then should you have any fear?

17. JOSEPH: It is something most terrible before the Lord,
     for a person should not give in to another man's wife,
     for if he does, then of his own volition
     he will stoke up against himself the fires of Hell which never
          go out.

18. WOMAN: Your sin shall be upon me, O Joseph;
     just follow me and carry out my desire,
     then I will do whatever you want,
     and your master will hold you in honour and revere you.

[The rest is lost.]

10. The Passover Lamb and the Exodus (Exodus 12, 14): Ephrem, Hymns on Unleavened Bread, 3

Introduction

In this exploration of the symbols, or "mysteries," hidden in the paschal lamb, Ephrem compares the achievements of the Passover lamb of Exodus and the Christ, the "True Lamb" and "Living Lamb" (cf. John 1.29). What the Passover lamb achieved on a historical level— the delivery of the Hebrews from the tyranny of Pharaoh—the True/ Living Lamb has achieved on two levels, the delivery of the Gentiles from Error in historical time, and the delivery of the dead from the dominion of Death in sacred time (for this theme, see further Ch. IV, no. 11). An analysis of the poem indicates that the typological patterns are carefully reflected in its very structure:

1.	Resemblances
2–3.	Comparison of achievements
4.	Differences (shadow: fulfilment)
5.	Old = single, New = double
6.	Passover lamb: Exodus of Hebrews from Egypt
7.	True Lamb: Exodus of Gentiles from Error
8.	Living Lamb: Exodus of Dead from Sheol.
9.	Egypt as a symbol for Sheol and Error
10.	Passover lamb: Egypt hands back the Hebrews
11.	Living Lamb: Sheol disgorges the Dead
12.	True Lamb: Error casts up the Gentiles
13.	Passover lamb: Pharaoh returns the Hebrews
14.	Living Lamb: Death returns the Righteous
15.	True Lamb: Error returns the Gentiles
16.	Pharaoh as a symbol for Death and Satan
17.	Passover lamb: Egypt breached
18.	True Lamb: Satan foiled
19.	Living Lamb: Grave emptied.

Translation

1. In Egypt the Passover lamb was slain;   Ex 12.6
   in Sion the True Lamb was slaughtered.

Refrain: Praise to the Son, the Lord of symbols
   who fulfilled every symbol at his crucifixion.

2. My brethren, let us consider the two lambs,
   let us see where they bear resemblance and where they differ.

3. Let us weigh and compare their achievements:
   of the lamb that was the symbol, and of the Lamb that is the
      Truth.

4. Let us look upon the symbol as a shadow,
   let us look upon the Truth as the fulfilment.

5. Listen to the simple symbols that concern that Passover,
   and to the double achievements of this our Passover.

6. With the Passover lamb there took place for the Jewish people
   an Exodus from Egypt, and not an entry.

7. So with the True Lamb there took place for the Gentiles
   an Exodus from error, and not an entry.

8. With the Living Lamb there was a further Exodus, too,
   for the dead from Sheol, as from Egypt.

9. For in Egypt a pair of symbols are depicted,
   since it reflects both Sheol and Error.

10. With the Passover lamb, Egypt's greed
    learnt to give back, against its wont;

11. With the Living Lamb, Sheol's hunger
    disgorged and gave over the dead, against its nature.

12. With the True Lamb, greedy Error
    rejected and cast up the Gentiles who were saved;

13. With that Passover lamb, Pharaoh returned the Jewish
       people,
    whom, like Death, he had held back.

14. With the Living Lamb, Death has returned
    the just who left their graves.   Mt 27.52

15. With the True Lamb, Satan gave up the Gentiles
    whom, like Pharaoh, he had held back.

16. In Pharaoh a pair of types were depicted;
    he was a pointer to both Death and Satan.

17. With the Passover lamb, Egypt was breached,
    and a path stretched out before the Hebrews.

18. With the True Lamb, Satan, having fenced off all paths,
    left free the path that leads to Truth.

19. That Living Lamb has trodden out, with that cry which he
         uttered,   Mt 27.50
    the path from the grave for those who lie buried.

11. The Veil of Moses (Exodus 34.33–35): Ephrem, Hymns on Faith, 8

Introduction

Ephrem was living at the time of the Arian controversy, concerning the relationship of the Son to the Father; in particular, which side of "the chasm" (as Ephrem called it) between Creator and creation should the Son be located? Ephrem (and Christian tradition in general) located him with the Father, whereas his theological opponents held that he was created, albeit before the rest of creation. One of the issues at stake was how humanity has knowledge of God. Since only what is *within* creation is capable of being investigated by the human mind, it made a great difference to which side of "the chasm" the Son belonged. Since Ephrem held that the Son is beyond "the chasm"—and indeed is the Creator himself—any idea that the human mind could investigate, or "pry into," his transcendent nature was not only utterly misguided, but also blasphemous. In order to make his point, Ephrem here offers a collection of *a fortiori* arguments based on various biblical passages, commencing with the episode of Moses' veil.

Translation

1. How great was the aura of Moses   Ex 34.29
   for no one was able to look on him;
   those who beheld were unable
   to gaze upon a mortal:
   who then will dare to gaze upon
   the Lifegiver of all, the Awesome?
   If a mere servant's aura
   has such power,
   who then will gaze upon his Master?
   Mount Sinai, when it saw him,   Ex 19.18
   issued forth smoke and melted before him!

2. The circumcised Jews were unable
   to look upon the glory of Moses: Ex 34.35
   the veil ministered
   between his aura and the people.
   In place of the veil that has grown old,
   brightness of Living Fire   Ezek 1.27
   surrounds the Chariot
   lest the cherubim be affrighted.
   But for you, let silence and quiet
   be your curtain,   Lev 16.2
   so that you gaze not upon his Aura.

3. No one approached the folds
   of that visible veil
   to pry into the aura
   of the servant, which resided within it.
   When Moses went to look,
   all the tribes quaked;
   how much more fearful is the search
   wherein any description of your nature lies hidden:
   if you just look upon the angel Watchers,
   the sky and the highest heavens
   tremble before you.

4. In the veil of Moses
   was your bright truth hidden;
   in his stuttering was hidden   Ex 4.10
   your eloquent instruction:
   beneath those two coverings
   were your truth and your utterance hidden.
   You lifted up the covering;   2 Cor 3.16
   you made plain the stammering:
   the whole of you came forth into the open,
   your truth speaking with a human mouth,
   your verity revealed to the eye.

5. The veil of Moses' face
   and the stammering of his mouth
   were two covers that covered over the blind People,
   but to the just you were revealed,
   to those who yearned for your day.   Jn 8.56
   The deniers, too, today
   are blind, with their eyes covered over;
   they stammer and only see dimly,
   blind to your beauty,
   muzzled in silence in response to your teaching.

6. He depicted parables to the foolish
    by means of Moses:
    thus two coverings   2 Cor 3.14–15
    were spread over the crucifiers.
    Truth has shone out in the open,
    so let us not grope in the dark;

    Gen 19.11; Deut 28.29; Job 12.25

    let us not have theological prying
    as a second veil:
    Beauty has come out into the open;
    do not compare him to Adam,
    for he resembles his Father in everything.

7. The priest used to enter
    the Holy of Holies in silence,
    and only once a year,   Lev 16.34; Heb 9.7
    going in with trepidation.
    If that Tent
    was so resplendent,
    who will make bold to pry
    into the Power that dwells within it?
    Let us accord honour
    in any enquiry into the Firstborn,
    for he is the Lord of the Sanctuary.

8. Two hundred and fifty priests   Num 16.2
    burnt incense in their censers,
    wanting to snatch away
    Aaron's priesthood.
    Thus the followers of Korah were swallowed up,   Num 16.31
    who wanted to act as priests.
    If Aaron's priesthood
    is so full of awe,
    how much more so is the Lord of priests

who officiated with his own blood?
Who will dare pry into him?

9. With a sudden mighty groan
    did the sons of Aaron get burnt up:
    they made bold and introduced
    extraneous fire;
    who then will escape
    the great fire,
    if he introduces into the church
    extraneous prying?
    There *is* enquiry in the church,
    investigating what is revealed:
    it was not intended to pry into hidden things.

10. Uzzah the head priest supported the Ark   2 Sam 6.6–7
    as it travelled–and met his destruction:
    what he was bidden, he failed to do,
    and what he was not bidden, he did.
    They bade him bear the Ark
    upon his shoulders,
    but he stretched out his hands
    to support the Power which supports all,
    imagining that the Ark
    was about to fall.
    It slew him as he supported it.

11. Do not accord honour to the Holy
    in an area in which you have not been instructed.
    Uzziah, who did so,   2 Chr 26.18
    found his own honour turned into shame.
    Do not, on the pretext of investigating truth,
    pry into and abuse the Firstborn.
    Do not imagine that Faith

is about to fall:
it supports those cast down.
Do not try to support it, like Uzzah,
lest it destroy you in wrath.

12. Tyrants, full of abuse,
honoured the Ark;
having experienced its power,
they venerated it with offerings.   1 Sam 6.4–5
Dagon was destroyed before it,   1 Sam 5.4
it cut off his limbs.
How much more should we honour the Gospel
before which the Evil One is destroyed,
cut off from his dominion!
Let us meet it with offerings,
seeing that it has healed our shattered state.

13. Again, the Jordan beheld the Ark   Josh 3.17
and divided itself:
the river whose course ran forward
fled and turned back,   Ps 114.5
flowing against nature
because it had seen the Lord of Nature.
If the Ark, with the Tables of the Law inside it
is so awesome,
how much more so is prying investigation into God?
Who will approach the place
wherein the Lord of the Tables is hidden?

14. Daniel beheld
wondrous beasts;   Dan 7.3
he also saw, seated in glory,
the Ancient of Days.   Dan 7.13
He approached the beasts

to ask questions and to learn: Dan 7.16
he did not draw near to the glory of the Exalted One
in order to investigate it.
Foolish men have now abandoned creatures
and rushed on to pry
into the nature of the Creator.

15. Daniel saw
    one of the angels and was perturbed.   Dan 8.16
    He did not approach to investigate:
    he was incapable of understanding its voice.
    Daniel was not able
    even to understand the angel's voice,
    nor did he see the one who ministers:
    who then will gaze upon him to whom the angels minister?
    The sea, when it saw his sign,
    took fright and fled; it stirred   Ps 114.5
    and was split into two parts.

16. Daniel, who enquired
    concerning the utterances,
    heard that they were sealed up and hidden.   Dan 12.9
    If it is not right to investigate
    what is hidden only for a time,
    who will dare investigate
    that treasury
    wherein resides all knowledge?
    The Firstborn is the Father's treasurer:
    all thought about the one depends on the other,
    so who may investigate him?

12. Elijah and the Widow of Sarepta (1 Kings 17): anonymous narrative poem

Introduction

The end of the drought imposed by Elijah's ban (1 Kings 17.1) is linked in this poem to Elijah's raising of the son of the widow of Sarepta (1 Kings 17.22), whereas in the biblical text God's promise of rain only occurs "after many days," in 1 Kings 18.1. The link made here, however, is known from both Jewish and other early Christian sources, and its origin evidently lies in the Jewish tradition concerning the three "keys," of birth, of rain, and of resurrection. According to this tradition, Elijah has been allowed by God to make use of the key of rain (specifically referred to in line 305 of the Syriac poem), but since Elijah then fails to remove his ban on rain and dew, God employs various stratagems whose aim is to change Elijah's zeal into pity. Elijah, however, remains unmoved—until finally, when the widow's son dies and she accuses him of being the cause of his death, he prays to God, asking for his resurrection: God complies—but only on condition that Elijah hand back the key of rain.

Translation

To the servant whom his master loves
does that master give authority over all he has,
but if it should happen that he turn against him,
then his master will deprive him of all that he has.
Elijah, whom his Master loved,   5
was given authority over both heights and depths:
he bound the heavens as he willed,
and on earth he did all that he pleased.
Elijah beheld the idols
being worshipped by his fellow men,   10

and his heart burned with zeal
at seeing the iniquity that was performed:
he saw the images being worshipped,
and the idols held in honour.
He raised his eyes to heaven   15
and addressed it with full authority:
"O heaven, it is to you that I speak,
the tent which is the bearer of blessings;
do not let down any dew or rain   1 Kg 17.1
until I bid you so to do.   20
Let us see what it is that men are worshipping,
whether it be God or idols;
and wherein lies advantage—
in the Creator, or in things created."
The heaven heard and was held bound: 25
all its functions came to an end;
lightnings and thunders disappeared;
all the clouds were hidden away.
A single word that had ascended from below
had full authority in the heights;   30
the heaven heard and was held bound;
it began to clamour to God:
"Indeed, Lord, I beg you,
I speak as a maidservant before you,
who is this earthborn person   35
with a key that hangs from his waist?
To my eyes he looks like a pauper,
and I thought he was just a beggar,
but at the single word he aimed at me
all my functions have come to a halt."   40
Our Lord answered in reply
to the heaven that had spoken thus:
"It is Elijah, son of sojourners,
whom I am not able to compel;

he has been a zealot ever since his youth,   45
and all that he commands I perform.
Be patient with me for a little,
and wait till I go down to visit him.
I will go on proposing to him reasons,
until he becomes reconciled with you.   50
He bound you, and he shall release you;
without him I shall not release you,
for if I release you without him
I will upset the priestly role:
lest one priest should bind,   55
and another should come along and release.
The same mouth of the priest who bound
shall be the one which releases."
Then along came God
and spoke to the prophet Elijah: 60
"What is this that you have done, Elijah,
holding back the heaven from giving rain?
Why did you prevent the rain
and not allow the dew to descend?
For with just one of these   65
both the seeds and the earth's fruit would grow;
but you have prevented both of them
from descending upon the fields.
If I do in accordance with your word,
who is going to provide food for you?   70
By your life, Elijah,
it is not a good thing that you have done,
for you have abandoned the whole of creation,
and you are concerned only with yourself.
Would it not have been easier for you to say,   75
O zealous Elijah,
that no dew or rain shall come down
until God gives the order?

But instead you have taken on airs and said
overboldly in your zeal,   80
'No dew or rain shall descend
until I give the order.'"
Elijah answered and said
to his Master who had spoken these things:
"Indeed, Lord, I beg of you,   85
speaking as a servant before you,
if I had said, 'Let it not descend
until God gives the order,'
then two or three upright people
would have got up and persuaded you."   90
Our Lord answered and said,
"Rise up and set off for the wadi Cherith: 1 Kg 17.3
it is a large and splendid wadi,
full of all sorts of good things;
its trees are extremely numerous,   95
and its fruits are very delicious;
its springs are abundant,
and it is superior to all other wadis."
This is the reason God sent him there,
in order that he might go and see it dried up,   100
and in his great grief he might be abashed
and unbolt the door that he had closed.
So the zealous man set off
for the wadi whither his Master had sent him;
he beheld its springs all dried up   1 Kg 17.7   105
and the animals dying,
but the cause of this did not occur to his mind,
and he did not open up the door he had closed.
Ravens, both evening and morning,   1 Kg 17.6
bring him food for his sustenance.   110
The sword of his tongue was drawn,
and he stood there and wandered among the trees,

embittered as he beheld
the wickedness and evil of the house of Ahab.
The trees heard how harsh   115
were the words of the prophet;
they bent their heads in obeisance to him,
like servants before their master.
God beheld the man
who had no compassion on his neighbour,   120
the Lord beheld the race of man
who did not spare his fellows,
and upon the crows he laid an ordinance
that they should not give him sustenance.
There was the first day, and they did not come,   125
and the second, and they were not there.
When he sees a crow flying
he gazes at its shadow:
"Young birds, what has seized you,
what has held you up, you who feed me?   130
Has some ill fate, maybe,
prevented you from coming to me?"
Hunger afflicted the prophet,
and his mouth became parched with thirst:
he got up and went to the fountain   135
to drink water in his thirst;
he bent down to drink from it,
but it swallowed up the water in front of him.
He sorrowed and was exceedingly grieved
by both hunger and thirst.   140
Elijah then spoke up and said,
"O hard-hearted earth,
with what rod can I strike you
that is better than the rods I have already used?"
And the earth groaned out like a bull: 145
"O man, who has held back water

from his own mother so that she cannot drink,
he who held back the crow from you
< [a line is lost] >
From whom are you asking milk?"   150
Then Elijah was pained
and called out to the Lord in grief,
saying in his sorrow,
"Lord, take my soul if you wish,
for I am no better than my forebears."   155
Then God answered
and spoke to Elijah as follows:
"Why are you grieved, Elijah,
calling me to come to your presence?
Have the crows caused you trouble,   160
and failed to serve you as they were bidden?"
Elijah answered and said,
"For two days I have not seen them."
And our Lord said in response
to the words of Elijah,   165
"you should realize, Elijah, what you have done;
if just a day or two's hunger
causes you such perturbation,
what should all creation do,
seeing that its children fade away from hunger?"   170
And he said to him after this:
"Rise up and go off to Sarepta near Sidon;   1 Kg 17.9
there I have bidden a widow
to see to your needs and to feed you."
So up got Elijah to go   1 Kg 17.10   175
to Sarepta of Sidon, whither he had been sent.
Then off he travelled, and he reached
the boundaries of the village;
and God, on the pretext of some wood,   1 Kg 17.10
brought out the widow to meet him.   180

Elijah beheld the widow
and began to say in his mind:
"I will ask her first of all for some water,
for water is available everywhere,
and from her words I will recognize her,   185
whether she is the one or not."
He approached and stood there before her,
he opened his mouth and addressed her:
"By your life, woman, bring me
a little water, for I am thirsty;   1 Kg 17.10   190
I am a foreigner passing by,
and I am tormented by thirst."
She went in to fetch him some water,   1 Kg 17.11
and then he turned round and asked her for bread,
but the woman replied and said   195
to Elijah after this:
"Are you a stranger to the world,
and have not heard what has happened?
There is a certain man called Elijah
who has held back the heaven from giving rain;   200
no one sows and no one reaps,
no one treads, and no one stores up.
The royal granaries are bare,
and are you asking a widow for bread?
No, by the Lord whom I worship,   205
your maidservant does not possess a thing,
beyond a little flour in a bowl   1 Kg 17.12
and a little oil in a horn.
And now I am gathering a couple of sticks
to make myself and my son some bread   210
so that we can eat and not die of hunger
in the affliction that is so strong in the land."
Elijah heard that there existed there
the name of the Lord whom he worshipped,

and he knew that this was the widow   215
unto whom God had sent him.
Elijah then said in reply
to the widow who had spoken thus:
"Neither shall the bowl of flour fail   1 Kg 17.14
nor shall the horn of oil give up."   220
The woman ran in
to test the word of the prophet;
she plunged her hand into the bowl—
and flour came leaping up to meet it.
She went next and uncovered the horn—   225
and out spurted oil from within it.
She kneads and makes bread
while her son carries in the wood.
Her son is exhausted by hunger
and asks her for some bread to eat.   230
His mother replied and said,
"Just be patient with me for a little:
let us first of all give the first portion to eat
to the person who gave us this flow,
and afterwards we ourselves shall eat   235
from this blessing with which he has benefited us."
Then she prepared and brought out to him
the food which his lips had asked for.
The man's heart was pacified,
with the result that he dwelt with the widow.   240
And the widow, with her only son,
flourished upon the earth—
but the earth remained in affliction,
while Elijah was reclining in ease.
Then the widow's son went out   245
with some boys, with bread in his hand.
The boys asked him and said,
"When there was plenty on the earth

you were dying of hunger;
but now that the royal storehouses are empty   250
you have bread—who gave it to you?"
The boy said to them in reply:
"My father had a friend,
and it was he who brought this bread."
The Lord looked upon the race of man   255
who failed to look on their companions;
God beheld a man
who had no compassion on his fellows,
and he sent an angel to take away
the soul of the widow's son.   1 Kg 17.17   260
He took away his soul, and so incited his mother
to do battle with the upright man:
the woman took hold of him and stood there,
ready to argue with him as a murderer.
"Give me back my only child," she said,   265
"for he was slain because of you.   cf. 1 Kg 17.18
I will straightway seize hold of you
and will cry out in my affliction,
as I cast you into the hands
of Ahab and Jezebel to meet an evil fate."   270
Elijah answered her and said
to the widow who had spoken these things:
"Never has anyone been killed by me,
and here you are calling me a murderer.
Am I God,   275
to be able to revive your son?
Or is his soul in my hands,
seeing that you are requiring him at my hands?"
The woman said in reply
to Elijah following this: 280
"Indeed, by the God whom you serve,
this is assured of me:

if the flour heard you and leapt up,
and if the oil heard you and spurted forth,
then the Lord will listen to you thus   285
and will give you back the soul of the boy."
Then Elijah took
the boy and brought him up to the upper room;   1 Kg 17.19
he knelt and began to say
in sorrow and suffering: 290
"Yea, Lord, I beg of you,   1 Kg 17.20
as a servant I speak in your presence;
why, Lord, have you requited with this loss
this widow who has received me?
Why did you send me to her,   295
why did you bring her son forth from her womb?
Lord, I call upon you with feeling,
I beg of you mercy;
listen, Lord, to your servant's prayer,
and return the soul of this boy."   1 Kg 17.21   300
Our Lord answered and said
to Elijah who had spoken thus:
"you owe me one debt:
repay it, and I will listen to you.
In your hands is placed the key to the heavens,   305
in my hands is the soul of the child."
The holy man opened his mouth
as his heart rejoiced and exulted;
he released the heaven which he had bound,   cf. 1 Kg 18.1
and the soul of the child returned.   1 Kg 17.22   310
His mother took him in joy
and gave praise to God,
while Elijah set off and went
with his heart rejoicing and exulting
because his Lord had answered his prayer,   315
and not held back the request of his mouth.

New Testament

1. The Angel and Zechariah (Luke 1.5–22): anonymous dialogue poem

Introduction

The poem is based on Luke's account of John the Baptist's father, Zechariah, and his encounter with the angel Gabriel when he went into the Temple to burn incense (Luke 1.9–20). Zechariah cannot bring himself to believe Gabriel's message, that his wife Elizabeth would bear a son, was true. The unknown author draws out in an imaginative way the brief dialogue to be found in the Gospel; he also adds one intriguing detail which is not in the Gospel text, although he does not exploit this any further: in the very first stanza it is stated that Zechariah entered the Holy of Holies to bring atonement for the people. This presupposes that Zechariah was High Priest (for only the High Priest could enter the Holy of Holies). Such an identification provides a date for the event, namely the Day of Atonement, 10th Tishri (approximately October), for it was only on that date that the High Priest could enter the Holy of Holies. The identification of Zechariah as a High Priest is already to be found in the second-century Protogospel of James, and some Syriac writers made use of it in order to work out the date of the Annunciation: with the help of Luke 1.26, which speaks of the coming of Gabriel to Mary as being in Elizabeth's "sixth month," this provides 10th Nisan (approximately April) as being the sixth month after Gabriel's message to Zechariah.

Translation

1. The feast came round for this Zechariah
    —the subject of our poem—
    to enter the Holy of Holies
    and bring atonement for his people.

    Refrain: Praise to you, O Lord,
    whom heaven and earth joyfully worship.

2. When Zechariah had entered before the Lord
    to fulfil his service
    by offering incense on the altar
    and partaking of atonement,

3. at that time he beheld an angel of the Lord   Lk 1.11
    who appeared to him
    to the right of the altar of incense
    —and he trembled in fear of him.   Lk 1.12

4. He saw him standing there, glorious
    and in great resplendence, and he trembled.
    The spiritual being approached,
    reassuring him with gentle and humble speech.

5. ANGEL: Fear not, Zechariah,   Lk 1.13
    for the occasion is good that has come to you:
    the Lord is pleased with your prayer,
    and has sent me to give you good tidings,

6. for the two of you, you and Elizabeth your wife,
    have done well before the Lord;
    and now she is pregnant and will bear you a child
    at whom you and many will rejoice.   Lk 1.14

7. No wine or strong drink shall he taste: Lk 1.15
    he shall be called the Lord's Nazirite.
    While still in the womb   Lk 1.15
    the Lord will fill him with the Holy Spirit and consecrate him.

8. John shall be the name of the fruit   Lk 1.13
    which Elizabeth shall bear;
    he shall clear a way before the Lord,   cf. Lk 1.17
    leaping before him as his messenger.

9. These are the words which Zechariah heard
    from the angel beside the altar,
    but he doubted at his presence
    and did not believe his message.

10. ZECHARIAH: How, sir, shall this be,
    that Elizabeth should have a child?
    She is old, and barren too;   Lk 1.18
    and I am old, as you can see.

11. ANGEL: The Watcher says: Listen, Zechariah,
    accept the message you hear from me:
    it is not difficult before the Lord
    for a barren old woman to give birth.

12. ZECHARIAH: We should compare a woman to the ground:
    when it is sown it produces a crop,
    but if it has totally failed to do so,
    there is no hope left for it: it will not produce.

13. ANGEL: For what reason do you doubt and not give
    credence?
    Why is it difficult for you to believe me?
    In the Lord's hands it is possible
    for something to be established out of nothing.

14. ZECHARIAH: It is patently impossible,
    as clear to me as the sun.
    She did not give birth when she was a young woman,
    so how can she do so in her old age?

15. ANGEL: I have revealed to you a mystery ordained by the
        Lord;
    I have told you, and you should not dispute.
    But if you do dispute it and fail to believe,
    then you should fear the judgement of him who has sent me.

16. ZECHARIAH: It would be astonishing if I were to believe
        you
    in the matter of this tale you have told me:
    a tree already dried up
    cannot possibly provide fruit.

17. ANGEL: You should realize, Zechariah, what a mistake you
        have made,
    you have not considered what has happened in the past;
    take the Scriptures and read in them
    of all the wonders the Lord has performed.

18. ZECHARIAH: It is certainly clear that the Lord is able,
    and I am convinced that such things have indeed taken place,
    but they were required by those times,
    and it was for that reason the Lord acted.

19. ANGEL: You know that the Lord has done these things
    and that they took place because they were required—
    but it is also because it is requisite now
    that Elizabeth is pregnant and will give birth.

20. ZECHARIAH: If these things took place in former ages
    it was because the world was young,

but now that it has grown mature
what is the need for a miracle?

21. ANGEL: If the world was not in need
of this miracle when it takes place
the Lord would not have sent me here,
and I would not have had to bring you the message.

22. ZECHARIAH: It is already harvest time
as far as I and Elizabeth are concerned;
there is no use for someone sowing seeds
when it is time for winnowing: that is quite out of place.

23. ANGEL: Yes, the harvest time has indeed arrived
as you have just said:
you will see a fruit for Elizabeth
and you will be filled with wonder when it happens.

24. ZECHARIAH: I can see that you are very glorious
and your radiance is more resplendent than that of anyone
     earthborn,
but however great and glorious you may be
I find your words hard to accept.

25. ANGEL: Take a look, Zechariah, and examine carefully,
look at Abraham from whom you descend:
he was an old man, and his wife
was barren as well, yet she gave birth.   Gen 21.2

26. ZECHARIAH: What you have told me about Abraham
is perfectly clear:
in that case it happened out of necessity,
so that his people might be blessed in his seed.   Gen 17.16

27. ANGEL: You are quite wrong, Zechariah, do not be so slow:
    the longer you hold out, the worse it will be for you.
    You would do better to believe,
    and so give praise to him who has sent me.

28. ZECHARIAH: The Lord knows he is hidden
    and all thoughts are revealed before him:
    even if I should accept your words with my lips,
    my heart is still unwilling to listen to you.

29. ANGEL: This day is the most glorious
    of all the days of the year for you both:
    in the same way your son shall be exalted
    above all the children born by women.   Lk 7.28

30. ZECHARIAH: However much you speak trying to persuade
        me,
    your words still do not reach my intellect:
    Elizabeth is smitten with two ills—
    old age and barrenness, both at once.

31. ANGEL: Likewise when the message was given to Sarah
                                          Gen 17.9–11
    these same two things applied—
    old age and barrenness together;
    yet because the Lord so willed it, she bore a son.

32. ZECHARIAH: Would that my intellect consented, sir,
    and that my doubt were uprooted;
    for it is quite clear to me that the Lord is able,
    yet I find it difficult to give credence to your word.

33. ANGEL: I wish you had never questioned it, Zechariah,
    you really should believe me;

Isaiah prophesied about your son   Is 40.3
long ago, as he was instructed.

34. ZECHARIAH: Who am I in this world
    to father the fruit he promised?
    However much you tell it me, I will not believe it
    because I know that it will not happen.

35. ANGEL: Your son shall be a messenger
    before the face of the Most High;   Lk 1.76
    he will clear a path before the Lord;   Is 40.3–4
    he will cry out and say, "Repent and turn back."   Mt 3.2

36. ZECHARIAH: I went up to the temple to please my Lord
    and offer incense before his altar;
    I did not realize I would hear in the temple
    these things that are quite beyond my ken.

37. ANGEL: I will proclaim a novel tiding to you,
    then maybe my words will be acceptable to you:
    I am Gabriel   Lk 1.19
    who serve before the Lord.

38. As long as you still do not believe what I have said
    and my words do not appear true in your mind,
    you shall be silent and dumb   Lk 1.20
    until these things have taken place in deed;

39. until Elizabeth gives birth
    and the child that issues from her is perfected
    your mouth shall be bound, without speech,
    and so will the gates of your ears, unable to hear.

40. Your mouth will be loosed only then,
    when all this that you have heard takes place;

and the gates of your ears will be opened   Lk 1.64
along with your tongue when it is loosed.

41. The angel expounded his message,
    bound him and left him in the temple—
    while all the people were astonished   Lk 1.21
    at his delay in the temple.

42. The crowd was thirsting with eagerness
    for Zechariah to come out from the temple.
    But when he did come forth, then they saw he was dumb;
    he motioned to them that he had seen a vision.   Lk 1.22

43. Entire Sion was amazed
    at what had happened to the upright priest.
    They understood that he had seen a vision,
    but what he had beheld they did not know.

44. They all stood up and stared
    while Zechariah, confident in their midst,
    indicated to them with his fingers
    the awesome vision seen by him.

45. Great is the tale he heard
    from the angel who had appeared to him,
    but he was unable to recount it
    and did not know how to convey it in signs.

46. They all put questions to him, but he could not hear,
    seeing that he was dumb, having lost his speech.
    They made signs to him to tell them what he had seen,
    even though he was unable to speak.

47. Astonishment reigned
    among the Hebrews at all this;

whether seated or standing,
their minds were occupied with the affair.

48. They were amazed and full of wonder
as they spoke to one another:
"What sort of son will this be,
when all this takes place at his conception?"

2. The Angel and Mary (Luke 1.26–38): anonymous dialogue poem

Introduction

Presented by the angel Gabriel with such an astounding message, Mary is portrayed in Luke's Gospel as being greatly troubled (Luke 1.29) and as questioning Gabriel (1.34). Building on this, the author of this poem explores what her inner feelings might have been, externalizing them in the form of a dialogue. Mary's wise questioning is contrasted explicitly with Eve's gullibility (verses 18–19) and implicitly with Zechariah's disbelief. It is significant that it is only when the angel mentions the Holy Spirit (in stanza 35) that Mary replies:

In that case, O angel, I will not answer back:
if the Holy Spirit shall come to me,
I am his maidservant, and he has authority.

Mary's openness to, and cooperation with, the Holy Spirit makes her response a model for all Christians.

As in the case of the poem for the Feast of the Annunciation (Ch. V, no. 1), Gabriel's message is described at one point (stanza 9) as a "letter."

Translation

1. O Power of the Father who came down and dwelt,
    compelled by his love, in a virgin womb,
    grant me utterance that I may speak
    of this great deed of yours which cannot be grasped.

2. O Son of the Bounteous One, whose love so willed
    that he reside in a poor girl's womb,
    grant me utterance and words
    that in due wonder I may speak of you.

3. To speak of you the mouth is too small,
    to describe you the tongue is quite inadequate;
    voice and words are too feeble
    to relate your beauty, so please bid me tell of you!

4. Grant that I may approach, O Lord of all,
    in awe to that exalted place
    of the chief of the angels when he announced
    to the young mother your coming.

5. You who are discerning, come, listen and give ear
    to this episode so entirely filled with wonder.
    Sing glory to him who bent down
    to give life to Adam who had sinned and so died.

6. The Father in his mercy beckoned to his Son
    to go down and deliver what he had fashioned,
    and to Gabriel the angel he gave instructions
    to prepare the path before his descent.

7. With David's daughter did Mercy shine out,
    for she was to be mother of him

who had given birth to Adam and to the world,
and whose name is older than the sun.

8. That Will which cannot be reached flew down
to summon the angel, sending him out
from the angelic hosts on his mission to her
to bring glad tidings to a virgin pure.

9. A letter did he bring, that had been sealed
with the mystery that was hidden from all ages;
he filled it with greeting to the young girl,
and fair hope for all the worlds.

10. Down flew the fiery being until he reached
the destitute girl, to fill her with wealth;
a greeting did he give her, announcing to her too
concerning her conception, the cause of wonder to all.

11. ANGEL: To the Virgin did the angel thus say:
Peace be with you, O mother of my Lord,   Lk 1.28
blessed are you, child,
and blessed the Fruit that is within you.   Lk 1.42

12. MARY: Says Mary: Who are you, sir?
And what is this that you utter?
What you are saying is remote from me,
and what it means, I have no idea.

13. ANGEL: O blessed of women, in you has it pleased
the Most High to dwell; have no fear,
for in you has Grace bent down
to pour mercy upon the world.

14. MARY: I beg you, sir, do not upset me;
you are clothed with coals of fire: mind you don't burn me.

What you have said is alien to me;
I am quite unable to grasp what it means.

15. ANGEL: The Father has revealed to me, as I do so now to
        you,
    this mystery which is shared
    between him and his Son, when he sent me to say
    that from you will he shine out over the worlds.

16. MARY: You are made of flame, do not frighten me;
    you are wrapped in coals of fire, do not terrify me.
    O fiery being, how should I believe you
    when all you have spoken to me is totally new?

17. ANGEL: It would be amazing in you if you were to answer
        back,
    annulling the message which I have brought to you
    concerning the conception of the Most High,
    whose will it is to dwell in your womb.

18. MARY: I am afraid, sir, to accept you,
    for when Eve my mother accepted
    the serpent who spoke as a friend,
    she was snatched away from her former glory.

19. ANGEL: My daughter, he certainly did use deception
    on your mother Eve when he gave her the message,
    but I, just as certainly, am not deceiving you now,
    seeing that it is the True One by whom I have been sent.

20. MARY: All this that you say
    is most difficult, so do not find fault with me,
    for it is not from a virgin that a son will appear,
    nor from that fruit, a divine being!

21. ANGEL: The Father gave me this meeting with you here
    to bring you greeting and to announce to you
    that from your womb his Son will shine forth.
    Do not answer back, disputing this.

22. MARY: This meeting with you and your presence here is all
         very fine,
    if only the natural order of things did not stir me
    to have doubts at your arrival
    about how there can be fruit in a virgin.

23. ANGEL: The angelic hosts quake at his word:
    the moment he has commanded, they do not answer back;
    how is it then that you are not afraid
    to query the thing which the Father has willed?

24. MARY: I too quake, sir, and am terrified,
    yet, though I fear, I find it hard to believe,
    since nature itself can well convince me
    that virgins do not ever give birth.

25. ANGEL: It is the Father's love which has so willed
    that in your virginity you should give birth to the Son.
    It is appropriate you should keep silence, and have faith too,
    for the will of the Father cannot be gainsaid.

26. MARY: Your appearance is venerable, your message full of
         awe,
    your flames are leaping up.
    Into the person of your Lord one cannot inquire,
    but that I should believe all this is difficult to me.

27. ANGEL: It is glad tidings that I have brought you:
    you shall give birth to your Lord, as I have explained.

O child, give thanks to him who has held you worthy
to be his mother, while having him as your Son.

28. MARY: I am but a girl and cannot
receive a man of fire.
The matter you speak of is hidden from me,
yet you proclaim that I should accept it.

29. ANGEL: Today for Adam hope has arrived,
for in you is the Lord of all pleased
to come down and release him, granting him liberty.
Accept my words, at the same time give thanks.

30. MARY: Today I wonder and am amazed
at all these things of which you have spoken to me.
Yet I am afraid, sir, to accept you,
in case there is some deceit in what you say.

31. ANGEL: When I was sent to announce to you
I heard his greeting and brought it to you.
My Lord is true, for so he has willed
to shine forth from you over the worlds.

32. MARY: All your words quite astonish me,
I beg you, sir, do not blame me,
for a son in a virgin is not to be seen,
and no one has ever slept with me.

33. ANGEL: He will come to you, have no fear;
he will reside in your womb, do not ask how.
O woman full of blessings, sing praise
to him who is pleased to be seen in you.

34. MARY: Sir, no man has ever known me,
nor has any ever slept with me.

How can this be, what you have said,
for without such a union there will not be any son.

35. ANGEL: From the Father was I sent
to bring you this message, that his love has compelled him
so that in you his Son should reside,
and over you the Holy Spirit will reside.   Lk 1.35

36. MARY: In that case, O angel, I will not answer back:
if the Holy Spirit shall come to me,
I am his maidservant, and he has authority;   Lk 1.38
let it be to me, sir, in accordance with your word.

37. ANGEL: Let your head be raised up, O maiden,
let your heart rejoice, O virgin;
O Second Heaven, let the earth   cf. Is 65.17
rejoice at you, for in your Son it acquires peace.

38. MARY: Let my head be raised up, sir, as you have said.
As I rejoice, I shall confess his name,
for if you, his servant, are so fair,
what might he be like? Tell, if you know.

39. ANGEL: This is something the angelic hosts are unable to do,
to gaze on him, for he is most fearful.
He is hidden within his Father's flame,
and the heavenly bands hold him in awe.

40. MARY: You greatly disturb me now,
for if, as you say, he is all flame,
how will my womb not be harmed
at the Fire residing there?

41. ANGEL: Your womb will be filled with sanctity,
sealed with the Hidden Divinity:

a place that is holy is greatly beloved
by God as a place where to appear.

42. MARY: O angel, reveal to me why it has pleased
    your Lord to reside in a poor girl like me:
    the world is full of kings' daughters,
    so why does he want me who am quite destitute?

43. ANGEL: It would have been easy for him to dwell in a rich
        girl,
    but it is with your poverty that he has fallen in love,
    so that he may become one with the poor,
    and enrich them once he is revealed.

44. MARY: Explain to me, sir, if you know this,
    when does he wish to come to me,
    and will he appear to me like fire
    when he resides in me, as you have said?

45. ANGEL: He has already so willed it, he is come and already
        resides in you:
    it was so as not to frighten you that you remained unaware.
    I dare not look upon you now
    that you are filled with the Fire that does not consume.

46. MARY: I should like, sir, to put this question to you:
    explain to me the ways of my Son
    who resides in me without my being aware;
    what should I do for him so that he is not held in contempt?

47. ANGEL: Cry out "Holy, Holy, Holy,"   Is 6.3
    just as our heavenly legions do, adding nothing else,
    for we have nothing besides this "Holy";
    this is all we utter concerning your Son.

48. MARY: Holy and glorious and blessed is his name,
    for he has looked upon his handmaid's low estate;　　Lk 1.48
    henceforth all generations in the world
    shall proclaim me blessed.

49. ANGEL: Height and depth shall sing out to him,
    angels and humankind shall give him praise,
    for he, the Lord of all, has come down
    and dwelt in a virgin, so as to make all things new.

50. MARY: Great is his mercy and not to be measured,
    far beyond what lips can describe;
    on high the heavens cannot contain him,
    yet below for him a womb suffices!

51. Let heaven and earth call him blessed;
    let both angel and virgin,
    and all humanity, too, call him holy,
    for in his love he has descended and become a human being!

52. Let heaven and angels give thanks on high,
    let earth rejoice in the Virgin;
    let both sides, as they exult,
    give praise to the Son of their Lord.

53. Let both sides be mingled in praise,
    both angels and humanity,
    to the Son who has restored peace between them,　Col 1.20–21
    when between them there had been anger and disruption.

54. Thanks be to you, Lord, from all the fiery
    and invisible worlds;
    in this world, too, from every mouth
    let the earth sing praises to you.

3. Mary and Joseph (Matthew 1.18–24):
anonymous dialogue poem

Introduction

The author of this vivid dialogue imagines what Joseph's feelings must have been, arriving home to find his fiancée pregnant by (as he naturally supposes) another man. Mary's explanations seem to him incredible, flying in the face of all reason. Mary's steadfastness eventually leads Joseph to agree to divorcing her (Matthew 1.19), at the same time promising he will not reveal the secret. In the next stanza (no. 34) Mary tells Joseph that the Child in her womb will himself reveal the truth of the matter, and Joseph finally concedes that there may, after all, be something in what she is saying. Once Joseph has reached this stage, where reason finally begins to allow that Mary's faith, as manifested by her persistence, may indeed have a firm basis, verification follows, in the angel's reassuring him in his sleep (Matthew 1.20).

Translation

1. Our Lord performed a wonder, my brethren,
   when he came down and resided in a Virgin–
   betrothed, chaste and excellent:
   her womb was sealed and her conception glorious.

Refrain: Praise to you, Lord, for at your coming
   sinners turned from their wickedness
   and entered into the protection of Eden's Garden,
   which is the holy Church.

2. An angel brought a greeting of peace and gave it   Lk 1.28
   to the daughter of poor parents, filling her with wealth;

she received a conception that astonishes everyone,
treating it in wonder.

3. In her womb was the child who fashions all,
   in her breasts was the milk which astonishes all.
   Her virginity was sealed, yet her womb was full;
   she was pregnant with child, but the secret was hidden.

   Mt 1.18

4. Joseph was dumfounded at Mary,
   seeing her pregnancy of which he knew nothing.
   He began to chide and reproach her,
   saying, Listen, young girl;

5. JOSEPH: Reveal to me the secret of what has happened to
   you;
   it is most shocking, what you speak of:
   who has led you astray, virgin,
   and snatched your wealth, chaste girl?

6. MARY: I will reveal to you how it happened,
   says Mary, So listen, Joseph.
   A man of fire came down to me,
   he gave me a greeting–and this took place.

7. JOSEPH: That I should believe this is hard:
   it is not nice, so do not repeat it.
   If you are willing, speak to me
   about what took place: who led you astray?

8. MARY: How to tell you any more I know not,
   for I have told you how it actually happened:
   the chief of the angels came down and announced it to me;
   I became pregnant without being aware of it.

9. JOSEPH: These words are inappropriate,
    Mary, for a virgin; keep silent,
    for falsehood will not stand up.
    Speak the truth, if you are willing.

10. MARY: I repeat the very same words—
    I have no others to utter.
    I remain sealed, as the seals of my virginity,
    which have not been loosed, will testify.

11. JOSEPH: You should not contradict,
    but confess that you have been seduced.
    Now you have fallen into two wrongs:
    after getting pregnant, now you tell lies.

12. MARY: You should believe my words,
    for you have never seen any falsehood in me:
    my chaste and truthful way bears me witness
    that I am a virgin and have not lied.

13. JOSEPH: I am astonished at what you say:
    how can I listen to your words?
    Virgins do not get pregnant
    unless they have intercourse or get married.

14. MARY: I am astonished that you will not believe,
    for it is very easy for the Lord of all
    to give fruit to a virgin—
    as happened with the lamb from the branch.   Gen 22.13

15. JOSEPH: Eve was married to Adam,
    and from him she had many children,
    whereas you alone brazenly assert
    that your womb is full without any man being involved.

16. MARY: Eve is actually a witness to my words,
    for she came into being without any intercourse,   Gen 2.21–22
    issuing from Adam who produced her as fruit.
    Why do you not believe me?

17. JOSEPH: You have gone astray like water, chaste girl;
    just take the Scriptures and read
    how virgins do not conceive
    without intercourse, as you are claiming.

18. MARY: You have gone astray, Joseph; take and read for
           yourself:
    in Isaiah it is written all about me,
    how a virgin shall bear fruit;   Is 7.14
    if that is not true, do not accept my word.

19. JOSEPH: It would befit you to be ashamed
    of the affair which is open to all;
    but now, after getting pregnant, you tell falsehoods,
    saying you are a virgin, to use your own words.

20. MARY: It would befit you, if only you were willing,
    to believe my words, for I am not telling lies.
    I remain sealed, as silent nature
    which has no voice testifies.

21. JOSEPH: Now you are glorying in falsehood
    which will not stand up, young girl.
    It is not possible in one and the same body
    for the seals of virginity to remain after conception.

22. MARY: Now you are causing me pain, Joseph,
    for I am pure, and there are witnesses:
    summon the local midwives
    and see how my seals of virginity have not been loosed.

23. JOSEPH: Do you know of anyone else like you,
    who resembles you, according to what you claim?
    To you alone has this happened—
    because it simply is not true.

24. MARY: I do not have to be like anyone else,
    for my Son has no fellow companion:
    he is unique, and it is not possible
    for another conception like mine to take place.

25. JOSEPH: So then something quite new in the world
    has started with you, or so you claim?
    You have no proof at all,
    and there is no explanation to what you say.

26. MARY: I have no fear of any "explanation":
    you have one to see, if only you would look.
    Who caused the stone on Horeb to flow with water,   Ex 17.6
    or who made that staff sprout forth fruit?   Num 17.8

27. JOSEPH: Let your mouth be silent, for your womb is full:
    it stands as your accuser, yet you have no fear!
    The very facts testify against you,
    and you will not even keep silent.

28. MARY: Let your mouth be silent and not pour blame on me,
    for I am not to be blamed in the eyes of anyone else:
    I am betrothed to you, as you are well aware.
    Do not let your idea of truth accuse me.

29. JOSEPH: It is very hard for me to believe you,
    that you have not exchanged me for another, as you are
        saying,
    for I know that I have no part in your conception,
    so it is quite apparent that you are telling lies.

30. MARY: It is very easy for you to believe me:
    my Son has one of the angels
    of fire and spirit who will testify in a revelation
    whether or not I am false.

31. JOSEPH: Actions cannot be done away with by words—
    and your words are opaque, while your womb is full:
    the very facts testify against you;
    your telling lies is quite unnecessary.

32. MARY: The cause of it is too hard for you or me to grasp,
    but it compels me, and so I speak.
    As long as my truthfulness is not impugned
    I will not bow my head or feel ashamed.

33. JOSEPH: There is error in your words, virgin,
    so that one is afraid for you after what you have said.
    Take the bill of divorce peacefully, and be off: Mt 1.19
    you may be sure I will not reveal the secret.

34. MARY: It is easy for the Child who resides in my womb
    to speak on my behalf when I am overcome;
    he will reveal the mystery that has happened to me;
    he will explain that I have not been false.

35. JOSEPH: Listen to what I shall say to you, O wise woman:
    though I believe what you say,
    I do not dare to touch
    your pure womb, for it is filled with fire.

36. MARY: Your utterance is dear to me, Joseph.
    I have no desire for intercourse:
    the Child in my womb will persuade you
    that I am a virgin and have not played false.

37. JOSEPH: There are two possibilities, and both disturb me:
    if it is true, it is most frightening for me,
    but if it is untrue, that is a great grief.
    How I wish I could escape from the two.

38. MARY: Now I shall pour out my words
    and address my Son hidden in my womb;
    he will reveal to you that I shall have no other children,
    and shall not be deprived of your company.

39. JOSEPH: Weighty is the matter you speak of,
    and I am afraid at what you say.
    All the more do I want
    to run away from you, being so distraught.

40. MARY: There will be a great commotion concerning me,
    and foolish people will hassle me;
    I shall be accounted an adulteress,
    and if my Son does not look after me I shall be torn to pieces.

41. Mary's Lord saw her truthfulness,
    and became a witness to her in her plight;
    he motioned to a ministering angel who came down
    and confirmed the young woman's words.

42. Joseph slept, and the angel arrived,   Mt 1.20
    revealing to him how the mystery had taken place.
    Joseph rose up early and knelt in worship   Mt 1.24
    before Mary, full of wonder, who had not lied.

43. The upright man in wonder at the young woman,
    honoured the virgin greatly.
    Thanks be to the Son who shone forth from her,
    who delivered both worlds at his birth.

44. Thanksgiving be to the Lord of all,
    said Joseph to the Virgin,
    in that of his will he has resided in your womb
    so as to give life to all at his nativity.

45. Thanksgiving be to him, and blessed be the name
    of the Word who resided in the Virgin,
    remaining nine months in her womb,
    so as to save Adam. All praises be to him!

4. Mary and Joseph (Matthew 1.18–24): anonymous narrative poem

Introduction

The starting point for this lively narrative is again Matthew 1.19, and Joseph's discovery of Mary's pregnancy. In order to indicate even more vividly what Mary will have suffered in the way of misunderstanding and abuse, the unknown poet also draws on the Protogospel of James, a work that was likewise popular in the medieval West. In this apocryphal Gospel of the second century we are told of Mary's childhood (which is only alluded to in passing in our poem) and how, when she was discovered to be pregnant, she was subjected to the ordeal described in Numbers chapter 5, the aim of the ordeal being to identify adulteresses.

The poem seeks to bring out the real danger in which Mary found herself as a result of her mysterious pregnancy (something which Mary herself is presented as acknowledging in stanza 40 of the previous poem), and the callous lack of sympathy on the part of her relatives, who are more concerned for the family's reputation than for her fate.

The author also alludes to two exegetical traditions which will be unfamiliar, since they are almost entirely confined to the Syriac tradition and its derivatives. In the first, in lines 132–3 where Mary adduces, as an instance in the Bible of a virgin birth, the tree which "gave birth to the lamb in place of Isaac" (Gen 22.13), has already been encountered (in Ch. III, no. 6, and IV, no.3).

In line 413 reference is made to Simeon who, as it becomes clear from lines 422–3, is the Simeon of Luke 2.25–35 who received the infant Christ in the Temple. From his request to be "released" in verse 29 (compare also 26), it has been widely deduced that he was of a great age. One strand of Syriac exegetical tradition went a step further and identified him with Simeon, the father of Jesus ben Sirach, author of Ecclesiasticus: this was done through supposing that the Syriac form of the name, bar Sira, was abbreviated from bar Asira, "son of the bound one"[1]—bound by being kept alive, and hence described as awaiting release in Luke 2.29.

Translation

Rumour went out over all Israel
that Mary the Virgin was pregnant with child.
Joseph heard and horror seized him,
he was sunken in great grief.
He left his work in the village   5
and directed his steps straight into the house.
As he went through the streets
he saw them all laughing at him:
he bent down his head as he wept
and entered his home, full of grief.   10
The holy girl came out to meet him,

---

[1]In the great seventh-century manuscript of the Syriac Old Testament in the Ambrosian Library, Milan, the author's name is actually given at the end as "bar Asira" (51:30). An excellent guide to the complex Syriac traditions surrounding Simeon can be found in J.F. Coakley's "The Old Man Simeon (Luke 2.25) in Syriac tradition," in *Orientalia Christiana Periodica* 47 (1981), pp. 189–212.

welcoming him with joy;
she darts hither and thither before his face
like the sun resplendent in its rays.
He raised his eyes and looked at Mary   15
as she stood there, clearly pregnant.
He had no idea what to say,
he was astonished to see her, and utterly perplexed.
When Joseph was about to rebuke her
his tongue just stuttered in his mouth;   20
he gazed on her filled with beauty,
completely astounded at her pregnancy.
Mary saw her betrothed,
and was saddened for his sake.
She began to speak in modesty,   25
saying gently in response to Joseph,
"Why are you so sad?
Why is your mind upset?
Someone who comes in from the road
usually displays a happy countenance,   30
and all those who live in his house, on seeing him,
come out to meet him with joy—
and I too rejoice to see you,"
says Mary to Joseph,
"and now I am begging you   35
to tell me all about your sorrow."
The chaste man began to speak
with the virgin filled with beauty.
He says to her with emotion,
relating to her the suffering of his heart,   40
"you were so beautiful in your chastity
and lovely in your purity—
all the tribes of Israel
called you blessed among themselves.
The priests, seeing your virgin state,   45

summoned me and gave me charge over your beauty,
telling me, 'Joseph, see to it
that you preserve Mary in purity.
Do not let any deceit enter your house,
and do not incur a curse in the House of Israel.   50
See to it, Joseph, that you do not incur guilt
in that sanctuary of God.'
So do you, Mary, take in my words
and tell me about the report that you are pregnant.
O Mary, where are your fair looks,   55
where is the beauty of your chastity?
Where is the light of your free choice?
O my beauteous one, who has stolen from you
and taken away the seal of your fair looks?
O Mary, did I not say to you,   60
'Guard your chastity and your true vocation,
stay in your holy way of life,
lest all who know you should jeer at you—
and call you a prostitute as well.'
I took off my five sons   65
so that they should not be a stumbling block for you.
O Mary, why have you forgotten
that conversation with the angel
who spoke with you in the sanctuary,
'Greetings to you filled with grace'?   70
For now I have been made today
into an object of reproach and mockery for my friends."
Mary saw that Joseph was weeping,
and her own tears flowed down in sympathy.
She explained the matter to Joseph,   75
"As the Lord lives,
I have not acted deceitfully before your love;
no, by the God of heaven,
I have not experienced any intercourse,

or done anything to transgress your bidding.   80
I have accepted betrothal to you,
my virginity is preserved, and I have known no man.
My God bears witness to heaven:
at about the ninth hour,
as I was standing in prayer,   85
a man of fire flew down;
I was frightened by his appearance,
but he greeted me and said,
'Greetings to you, Mary, my Lord is with you;   Lk 1.28
from you shall a Savior shine forth,   90
a deliverer for all creation.
And the Holy Spirit shall overshadow you.'   Lk 1.35
I said to him, 'How shall this be,
seeing that I do not know the marriage bed?'   Lk 1.34
He told me, 'Do not be perturbed,   Lk 1.30 95
O Maid filled with mercy and grace,
for the power of the Most High shall reside in you, Lk 1.35
the Sovereign shall shine forth from your womb;
his kingdom shall last for ever.'"   Lk 1.33
Joseph listened, and he was gripped by grief   100
at what he heard from her.
"Mary, spare your tongue,
do not blaspheme against God,
lest all the gentiles speak
about this blasphemy of yours against God;   105
the wickedness of our own house is quite enough;
do not let us add to our blasphemy.
O Mary, who will ever believe you,
that God has resided in your womb?
Who will give credence to your words,   110
that your pregnancy is not the result of intercourse?
O Mary, what woman
has ever given birth while still a virgin?

Who will ever believe this novel teaching?
The mind simply cannot accept it.   115
You have not been willing to reveal this man of yours,
you have cast an insult on God.
Keep quiet with the tale you have uttered,
take this man of yours, and be off in peace."
The Virgin wept on seeing the weeping   120
of Joseph, the upright and righteous.
The Virgin says to the blessed man,
"Listen to me, so that I may speak before your love.
I am preserved in my virginity
as on the day before I left my mother's womb;   125
I am sealed and preserved,
my God is witness in heaven.
And if you are investigating about the pregnancy,
come, I will show you what is written, Joseph:
Who ever has joined with the Earth   Gen 2.7   130
so that it bore Adam?
Who was married to the Tree
that it gave birth to the Lamb, in place of Isaac?   Gen 22.13
Again, how did the Rock give birth   Ex 17.6
to rivers of water in Ashimon?   Ps 78.16   135
And how did the donkey's jaw bone   Judg 15.19
cause water to flow for Samson?
O my lord Joseph, have you not heard
that the Rod sprouted for Aaron?   Num 17.8–9
All the mysteries which were administered   140
depict the mystery of the Messiah."
Chaste Joseph replied and said
to her who was full with what is holy,
"Do not repeat these things before me,
for their interpretation does not belong to you.   145
I kept you in chastity,
I gazed upon you with honour,

but I was not aware that there are people
who are laughing at your free choice.
What foolish deed has been at work   150
so that you have introduced adultery into my bed?
Alas, how much did I rejoice in you,
but now you have humiliated me today.
People point at me with a finger, saying,
'The harlot is in this man's house.'   155
Alas, Mary, for the time when they say to me,
'O fool, what is it that you have allowed to happen?'
Alas for the time when they require you at my hands,
blaming me for your pregnancy.
Your testimony does not apply to yourself: 160
why have you repeated to me those things that are written?
It is not instruction from the Scriptures
that your pregnant womb requires,
but rather that you should reveal the man
who has committed adultery with you; and that done,
    be off!   165
It has pleased you to debase your high estate;
farewell, then, to you and your man.
As for me, I shall never associate
at your table.
And if God has so willed and performed   170
signs in former times,
such things do not apply to you;
you have no one else in the world as precedent:
had just one woman conceived
without intercourse, as you say is the case with yourself,   175
then we might have reason to believe your claim
that women can give birth without intercourse.
The Tree does not resemble you,   Gen 22.13
nor do any of the other things which you have recounted.
The person who does correspond to you is the prostitute   180

who is stoned once she is found out.   Deut 22.21
May the Lord free me in his mercy
from the scandal your youthfulness has brought about;
but I was not aware of your having been corrupted,
and I had no idea of what had happened to you."   185
"Listen, my lord Joseph, and let me speak to you,
and do not reckon me among the prostitutes:
as the good Lord lives,
I have never experienced intercourse.
No, by the Lord who delivered Isaac   190
from the knife on the pyre;   Gen 22.10–11
no, by that Lord who delivered our people;
no, by that power of God
which descended upon Mount Sinai,   Ex 34.5
I assure you I have had no knowledge of any man   195
from the very day I was born.
No, by the Lord of Joshua, son of Nun,
who routed thousands and tens upon thousands,
I have had no experience of intercourse
such as is the norm with females   200
and with women, just as you have said.
Do not hold me to be false, Joseph, my lord;
spare my young age, do not let me die:
all that I say is true,
there is no falsehood in my words at all.   205
Look, there are wise women in our locality
who know the manner of females:
they can testify to my free state,
that I am untouched by intercourse."
Mary wept when she saw   210
how Joseph, the upright and just, wept.
The Lord heard from within her womb
the sound of her bitter weeping.
She raised her eyes on high,

and saw how the heaven was perturbed: 215
as he resided in his mother's womb
creation trembled at him.
An angel of fire flew down,
Gabriel, the chief of the angels;
he left the Most High and descended, 220
and reassured the upright Joseph, Mt 1.20
telling him, as he gave him comfort,
the whole truth, just as it was.
Joseph arose from his sleep, Mt 1.24
bowed down before Mary as he gave praise 225
to the Lord who had composed his distracted mind,
dispelling the doubt of his thoughts,
turning his heart to the truth,
reassuring him through Gabriel.
Then, following all this, 230
the messenger from the priests arrived, saying,
"Bring Mary along to the assembly;
come and see the priests who are summoning you."
Joseph arose and took with him Mary.
The crowds thronged to catch sight of her; 235
the daughters of Israel and her companions spat on her face in
    the streets;
the noble born of her family, too,
reviled her amidst cries of lament,
"Alas for our fair name,
how it has perished this day! 240
Alas, for in you our family is put to shame
amidst the tribes of Israel.
Alas for your chastity—who soiled it?
Alas for your virginity—who has destroyed it?
Alas, for how proud we were of you, 245
but now our heads bow at your fall.
Alas for us henceforth and for ever,

for our fair name has perished."
When Mary heard these words
and saw that everyone was reviling her,   250
she ceased gazing up to heaven,
and gazed instead towards her womb,
"My Lord, you wished it, and I have become your mother;
bid that this uproar concerning me be stilled,
for the shadows of death have encircled me   cf. Ps 55.5   255
at the sound of those who revile me."
When her tears reached her womb
as she wept bitterly,
that Power who resided within her stirred
and commanded that her raiment become fire: 260
lightning struck out beneath her;
her face gleamed out just as the sun
when it shines forth in the morning.
The priests beheld her in amazement.
Joseph approached, with Mary beside him,   265
towards the priests who quaked before her.
They had wanted to speak harshly,
but their tongues were tied;
the sound of their words left them
at the amazement that had overtaken them.   270
Gently and quietly
did they speak with her, saying,
"You know, Mary, that it was as the result of vows
that God gave you to your mother,
and you were brought up in the Temple   275
like an offering without blemish.
Your mother gave instructions the day she died, saying,
'Take Mary carefully.'
God saw her prayer,
and he hearkened to the voice of her request.   280
And the Levites held blessed

your chastity and virginity;
the angels of heaven cherish you,
and a salutation of peace descended upon you.
You have eaten the bread of heaven,   285
you have received the company of an angel.
But now, Mary, tell us,
who has mockingly taken off your freedom?"
Mary wept as she heard this,
and she spoke to the priests with suffering,   290
"I beg of you, accept what I have to say,
and do not reckon me an adulteress.
I am a virgin, and have known no one:
God bears witness to this,
I am preserved and am still sealed;   295
the seal of my youth is intact.
Examine and see that I have not been laughed at,
spare me, and accept my words.
I received a salutation from on high,   Lk 1.28
from the Father at the hands of a messenger;   300
while I was standing in prayer,
he greeted me and addressed me thus,
'My Lord is with you, from you shall he shine forth.'
At his utterance I was terrified,   Lk 1.29
but by his peaceful salutation he calmed me,   305
giving me courage as he spoke as follows,
'The Power of the Most High will overshadow you, Lk 1.35
and the Holy Spirit will reside in you;
and as for the Son who shall be born from you,
his kingdom shall last forever.'"   Lk 1.33 310
The priests and chief priests heard,
and astonishment settled upon them;
they were amazed at her beauty,
and her words were weighty too.
The narrative concerning her baffles the wise: 315

what degree of wonder can suffice for it?
Our Lord is glorious among his heavenly legions,
yet hidden in the womb of her who bore him!
In fear they spoke with Mary
whose entire story belongs to God.   320
The priests replied and said
to Mary, the holy Virgin:
"Of the water that God has given
through Moses to Israel,   Num 5.11–28
whosoever drinks of it having committed adultery   325
his belly will become inflated and burst;   Num 5.22
his thighs too will waste away,
and he will become an object of fear to those who behold it.
If you drink of this water
and it does you no harm, then you are innocent.
                                        Num 5.28   330
So it is now up to you, Mary,
whether you drink it or not."
Mary says, "I will drink it,
putting my confidence in God.
I stand here confidently   335
for I have not played the harlot or committed adultery.
Let the water of testing be my witness
among the people of Israel;
through it God shall give me
victory amidst the crowds.   340
Through it the people will be put to shame,
those who say that Mary has played the harlot."
When she approached to drink
of this water of testing,
the women, her kinsfolk, shook with fright   345
and implored her not to drink:
"Take our gold and our jewellery;
give a bribe to the priests, and thus escape;

lest some from the house of Israel should say to us,
"From you she received her harlotry"; 350
lest the gentile families should mock you
and laugh once again at you.
Let our family not be humiliated because of you;
let our name not be reviled in you;
let it not be abased through your humiliation 355
or at your life which will wear itself out in Sheol.
O Mary, take the man whom you have known,
go off in peace, and do not die."
To these words she paid no attention,
that pure bearer of God; 360
rather, she pressed forward to drink,
just as sheep do on a summer day.
She took the water of testing—
and all who beheld her were sorrowing.
But our Lord assisted the young girl, 365
giving the victory to her person.
After she had drunk the water
she went up to the mountain tops.
Lamentations accompanied her
as her kinsfolk wept for her, 370
as though for some dead person on his journey to Sheol,
one saying to another,
"Let us prepare clothes for the burial
of her whose death is at hand."
One was bringing a garment, 375
another prepared the perfumes;
and all the womenfolk of her family
began to weep as follows,
"How will it be when the beloved girl
rots away and is wrapped in a shroud? 380
What hands will lay hold
of the wretched girl whose flesh is consuming away?

Alas, how did her mother weep for her
as she left this world:
"The sorrow is not because I am dying,   385
for I know that all must die;
I sorrow for the sake of Mary,
whom I am abandoning in her youth.
But, my sisters, as you live,
take good care of her."   390
Had she been living today
and seen what has befallen her daughter
great would have been her pain and lamentation,
and who would have been able to comfort her?"
Everyone was weeping for the girl,   395
but she was rejoicing along with the angels.
Evening came, and she set off to descend,
while angels escorted her and greeted her.
All the peoples and nations
accompanied her in honour.   400
The priests saw her and were amazed,
for torches of light shone forth from her,
and the beauty of her face blazed out
like the fair-rayed sun.
All the upright went eagerly to meet her,   405
as though she had returned from the dead.
The priests knelt down in obeisance to her,
bowing their heads before her.
In amazement one spoke to the other,
"Great is this wonder   410
which we have seen today in this girl."
Simeon speaks before the people, saying,
"Listen, as I tell you this matter—
what I beheld in a revelation.
When I was in the land of Babylon,   415
weeping because of our people

and making supplication to God
for our salvation,
the Lord showed me, through the Spirit, saying,
"Simeon, why are you grieved?   420
For death cannot touch you   Lk 2.26
until you behold the Messiah."
And for five hundred years I have been bound,
awaiting this day.
Perhaps the Messiah will shine forth   425
for me to see, and then I will find rest in peace,
and in you, Mary, all things will find fulfilment,
for I know that your child is the Savior.
Where is the wisdom of the wise,
the knowledge of the mighty?   430
For they are put to shame in their wisdom,
while for you there has turned out to be victory."
From all sides came acclamations
of people kneeling before her in obeisance;
from all sides the cries of joy,   435
of exultation, and songs of praise.
All chaste women cried out,
"Welcome, O Bride of Light;
welcome, beloved one who have grown great.
Blessed is he who has given you victory!   440
Welcome, O Mary;
proceed to your dwelling where you were brought up;
call Joseph the upright, your betrothed,
for you are chaste in your purity,
like your holy Lord.   445
We beg of you, forgive us
the insults we hurled at you;
do not curse us, O daughter of David,
for we did wrong in ignorance.
Come in peace to Joseph,   450

and we will testify that you are a virgin;
you are pure, and the angels bear witness;
you are a virgin, and your womb is witness
that your Son will save all creation."
Joseph knelt in obeisance before her   455
and he sang out in acknowledgement,
"Come with me, beloved of God,
enter the abode of your betrothed.
Forgive me my wrong, O daughter of Light,
far be it from me I should have doubts over you any more.   460
I will proclaim without any shame
that you are a virgin, despite your conception,
and your Child will save all creation
from the error of idolatry."
They scattered perfumes before her feet,   465
and she walked on garments through the street.
The crowds thronged in her honour,
saying, "Come in peace,"
and the people, from end to end, cried out,
"Cursed is the mouth that reviles you;   470
accursed by the Lord of the Law
shall be all who call you an adulteress."
Praise be to God in the height
who wished to save all creation.
Blessed is the Lord in the height,   475
for whom your womb became a chariot.
Praise be to him and to the Father who sent him,
and to the Holy Spirit, halleluiah,
while upon us be mercy and compassion
at all times, amen and amen.   480

5. Mary and the Magi (Matthew 2.11): anonymous dialogue poem

Introduction

After some introductory stanzas the dialogue opens with a dramatic and paradoxical backdrop: the Magi, "chiefs of Persia," turn up, after a long journey, bearing expensive gifts for a child of a mother who is living in destitution. Mary cross-questions them, and suggests they have come to the wrong place. The Magi, however, have complete confidence and faith in the star that has led them, and they assure Mary that they are not mistaken. Only in stanza 28 does Mary give a hint that she is well aware why they have come, and in the following verses she expresses her fears that Herod will get to hear of it and there will be bloodshed (an allusion to the slaughter of the innocent children, Matthew 2.16). Eventually, towards the end (from stanza 40 onwards), Mary shares with the Magi her own secret, the angel Gabriel's message to her, and her virginal birthgiving.

Two references to Christ require explanation. In stanza 27 the Magi refer to the child as "the Ancient of Days," alluding to Daniel 7.13. In the Aramaic original, as well as in the standard Syriac translation, the Ancient of Days is distinct from the "Son of Man," mentioned earlier in the verse. Accordingly Ephrem and other early Syriac writers take the Ancient of Days as referring to the Father. In the Old Greek translation of Daniel, however, the "Son of Man" is described as being "like (or: as) the Ancient of Days," thus allowing for the latter to become a title referring to Christ, rather than to the Father. This understanding is widespread in early Christian writings (and is also found in medieval eastern Christian art); knowledge of it will have reached Syriac writers through translations of Greek patristic literature, and from the fifth century onwards it is widely found, especially in liturgical poetry.[2]

[2]For this feature, see further my "The 'Ancient of Days': the Father or the Son?," *The Harp* (Kottayam) 22 (2007), pp. 121–30.

In stanza 34 Mary refers to her child as a "sweet cluster," which alludes to Isaiah 65.8, which had already been taken as a reference to Christ by Aphrahat in the fourth century, in his final Demonstration, which is specifically devoted to the christological interpretation of the verse.

Translation

1. At the birth of the Son, light shone out
    and darkness fled the world;
    the universe lit up in praise
    of the Father's Radiance who had illuminated it.

Refrain: Praise to you, Lord, at whose coming
    sinners turned from their wickedness
    and entered into the protection
    of the Garden of Eden, which is the holy Church.

2. He shone forth from the Virgin's womb,
    and shadows vanished as he appeared:
    darkness and error were suffocated thereby,
    while earth's extremities were illumined in praise.

3. Among the Peoples a great commotion arose
    for light had shone out in the dark.
    The Peoples leapt up in joyous praise
    of him whose birth had given them light.

4. As his light flashed forth over the East
    Persia was illumined by the star
    which came down bearing her an invitation
    to come to the Epiphany that gladdens all.

5. The luminary speeded on its way to shine out
    amongst those in dark, summoning them
    to accompany it and take pleasure
    in the great Light who had come down to earth.

6. A single messenger—the star—came down   Mt 2.2
    to announce and proclaim the glad tidings
    to the people of Persia, bidding them prepare,
    for the King whom they should worship had now shone
        forth.

7. Glorious Assyria, once it was aware,
    summoned the Magi, instructing them:
    "Take offerings and go to honour
    the great King who has shone forth in Judah."

8. The chiefs of Persia, in great delight,
    carried offerings from their own land
    to bring to the Virgin's Son
    gold, myrrh, and frankincense.   Mt 2.11

9. They entered to find him a young baby
    living in a poor woman's house.
    They knelt down in joyful adoration   Mt 2.11
    as they offered him their treasures.

10. MARY: To what purpose are these? Mary said,
    Why, and for what reason
    are you come from your own country
    with your treasures for this baby?

11. MAGI: Your son is a king, the Magi replied;
    he wears the crown and is Lord of all;
    his rule extends over the world,
    and all are subject to his sway.

12. MARY: When has it ever happened
    that a poor girl has given birth to a king?
    I am destitute and needy:
    how can a king appear from me?

13. MAGI: With you alone has this happened,
    for in you a great king shall appear.
    Through him your poverty shall make good,
    for crowns, O Mary, shall be subject to your son.

14. MARY: I have no royal treasure-house,
    I have not ever met with wealth.
    The house is poor and the dwelling bare;
    do not, O Magi, keep on telling me my son is a king.

15. MAGI: Your son is the great treasure-house
    containing wealth sufficient to make all rich.
    Other kings' treasure-stores may be reduced to poverty,
    but his will never run out or need to be rationed.

16. MARY: Maybe it is another king that you are talking about,
    born somewhere else: go and find out,
    for this is but the child of a poor girl
    who is unfitted to look on a king.

17. MAGI: How could we ever lose our way
    once the light was provided?
    It was not darkness that bade us leave,
    but we have travelled in light: your son is the king.

18. MARY: You can see the baby lying quiet
    and his mother's house, destitute and bare:
    there is nothing regal here—
    how can a king be seen here?

19. MAGI: Yes, we have seen the child lying there
    quiet in gentle humility, as you say,
    but we have seen too that he illumines the stars,
    so that they announce him on high.

20. MARY: You should enquire of different people
    to find out who is the king, and then pay him homage.
    Maybe the path's direction has changed,
    and the king is some other child who has been born.

21. MAGI: My girl, you should accept this,
    for we have learnt that your son is king for certain.
    He directed us on a smooth path
    by means of a bright star, one that is not transient.

22. MARY: The child is small; he has
    no royal crown or throne.
    What is it that you see, so that you offer
    your treasures as though to a king?

23. MAGI: He is small because he so willed it:
    the child is gentle and of low estate—until he is revealed:
    then will come the time when every crown
    shall be bowed down in worship of him.   cf. Phil 2.10

24. MARY: My son has no army
    or serried legions at his beck;   cf. Mt 26.53
    he is content with his mother's poverty.
    Why should he be proclaimed king by you?

25. MAGI: Your son's army is aloft,
    riding on high, all aflame,
    and ever since one of them came and summoned us
    our whole region has been astir.

26. MARY: The child is but a baby; how is it possible
    he should be king over all the world?
    How can a mere toddler
    govern mighty men and renowned?

27. MAGI: Your child is old, young girl,
    the Ancient of Days, prior to all others   Dan 7.13
    Adam is younger by far than he,
    and by him all creation is governed.

28. MARY: It would be best if you would explain
    and throw light on all this affair.
    Who has revealed to you this secret concerning my son,
    that he is king in your country?

29. MAGI: It would be best if you would just accept it,
    for if it were not the truth that we have brought,
    we would never have come laden all the way here
    from the ends of the earth for the sake of your son.

30. MARY: This whole secret, and what happened to you
    there in your country,
    please disclose it to me, like good friends:
    who summoned you to come to me here?

31. MAGI: A great star appeared to us,   Mt 2.2
    more glorious by far than the rest.
    Our land was enflamed with its light
    as it proclaimed that the King had shone forth.

32. MARY: I would not like you to tell all this
    in our country lest the local kings
    get to hear of it and become incensed
    with the child, out of envy.

33. MAGI: Do not be disturbed, young girl:
    your son can topple all crowns
    and place them beneath his feet.
    They cannot harm him, even if they get envious.

34. MARY: It is because of Herod that I am perturbed,   cf. Mt 2.3
    lest that mad dog upset me
    by unsheathing his sword
    and cutting off this sweet cluster before it is ripe.   Is 65.8

35. MAGI: Of Herod there is no need to fear;
    his throne lies in your child's hands:
    one nod and his crown will totter and fall;
    he will be destroyed, and that is the end of the wretch!

36. MARY: Jerusalem will be a torrent of blood   cf. Mt 2.16
    as lovely children are disfigured by him;
    if the city gets to know of it, people will make a dash for him.
    Let our talk be in secret: do not cause a disturbance.

37. MAGI: All torrents and awesome gorges
    will be tamed by your son.
    Jerusalem's sword will be blunted,
    and, unless he so wills it, your son will not be killed.

38. MARY: Jerusalem's scribes and priests
    are well instructed in matters of blood:
    should they discover, they would stir up murderous feuds
    directed at me and the child. O Magi, please do keep quiet.

39. MAGI: These scribes and priests have no power
    to harm your son in their envy:
    by him is their priesthood dissolved,
    their festivals annulled.

40. MARY: An angel revealed to me when I conceived the child
    that my son will be a king   Lk 1.32–33
    whose crown is exalted, never to be removed.
    He intimated to me just as you have said.

41. MAGI: That angel, then, of which you speak
    must be the one who summoned us, looking like a star.
    He was shown to us, so that we might announce to you
    that your son is greatly more glorious than the stars.

42. MARY: That angel who appeared to me
    explained to me, when he announced it,
    that his kingdom would have no end,   Lk 1.33
    but I kept it a secret, so that it might not be revealed.

43. MAGI: That star, too, explained to us
    how your son would wear the crown.
    Its appearance was different,
    for it was an angel, though it never told us so.

44. MARY: When the angel announced this to me
    he called him his Lord, even though he had not yet been
        conceived;   Lk 1.28
    he proclaimed him to me as the Son of the Most High,

                                                         Lk 1.32

    but where his Father is, I have no idea.

45. MAGI: The star too proclaimed to us
    that he who is born is the Lord of the heights:
    your son rules over the luminaries
    and without his orders they do not shine.

46. MARY: I will reveal before you a further secret
    so that you may be reassured:

I gave birth to my son in virgin wise.
Since he is God's Son, go and proclaim him as such.   Lk 1.35

47. MAGI: That star has already taught us
that he is God's Son and is Lord.
Your son is above all things,
he is Son of God, as you say.

48. MARY: The heights and depths testify concerning him,
along with all angels and stars,
that he is Son of God and Lord.
Convey the news of him to your country.

49. MAGI: The heavenly sky, by means of one star,
put Persia into commotion, and she has believed
that your son is the great King
to whom all nations are subject.

50. MARY: Convey back peace to your lands;
may prosperity abound in your realm.
O apostles of truth, may you be believed
in every place that you travel through.

51. MAGI: The peace of your son shall convey us
safe back to our country, just as we came.
When his rule takes hold of the world,
may he visit our land and sanctify it!

52. MARY: May Persia rejoice at the tidings you bring;
may Assyria exult at your arrival.
Once the kingdom of my son has shone out,
may he place his standard in your land!

53. Let the Church exult and sing
praise at the birth of the Most High,

for both heights and depths stand illumined at his Epiphany.
Blessed is he at whose birth all receive joy!

6. John the Baptist and Christ (Matthew 3.14–15): anonymous dialogue poem

Introduction

Of the four Gospels only Matthew gives a short dialogue between
John the Baptist and Christ before John baptizes him. It is this which
serves as the starting point of the Syriac dialogue. A number of motifs
characteristic of the Syriac tradition are to be found; in particular,
Christ is presented at the occasion of his Baptism as a Bridegroom
(based on Gospel passages such as Matthew 9.15 and parallels, John
3.29), and his Baptism is seen as his marriage to his bride, the Church
(stanzas 4, 23), the bride already having been betrothed (stanza 23),
and the bridal chamber prepared (stanza 12). This is a theme found
especially in the verse homily of Jacob of Serugh on Christ's Baptism,
while elsewhere Jacob uses it in connection with the pierced side of
Christ (John 19.34) where the blood and water which issue are seen
as the Church's sacraments of Eucharist and Baptism, so that Jacob
can speak of the Church as the Bride of Christ who is born from
his very side. Although Christ's Baptism and the piercing of his side
on the cross are totally separate in historical time, their combined
salvific content brings them together in sacred time, and so there
is no contradiction in the application of wedding imagery to both
events.

As in some of the hymns included in the next chapter, Christ's
Baptism is understood as one of the two main fountainheads for
Christian Baptism, and several stanzas specifically point forward to
that (notably stanzas 7, 24, 26, 32, and 38).

A further feature that is characteristic of Syriac liturgical poetry
is the description of Christ as Fire (stanzas 11, 29, 33–34); this will

also be a prominent feature in a poem of Ephrem's translated in the next chapter (V, no. 10).

Translation

1. My imagination wafted me to the Jordan
    where I beheld a wonder
    when the glorious Bridegroom was revealed
    to make a marriage feast for the Bride and to sanctify her.

    Refrain: Praise to you, Lord, whom heaven and earth worship in
    joy.

2. I saw John, filled with astonishment,
    with crowds standing around him,
    while the glorious Bridegroom bent down
    before the child of barren parents to be baptized.

3. My mind was amazed at both Word and Voice:
    John was the Voice,   Is 40.13 = Mt 3.3
    our Lord, who shone forth, was like the word
    ready to come out into the open, having been hidden.

4. The Bride was betrothed, but she knew not
    who was the Groom she was to expect.
    The wilderness was filled with the wedding guests assembled,
    and hidden among them there was our Lord.

5. It was then that the Bridegroom revealed himself,
    coming to John by the river.
    The herald trembled as he announced,
    "Here is the Groom whom I have been proclaiming." cf. Jn 3.29

6. There came to Baptism he who baptizes all,
    manifesting himself by the Jordan.
    John beheld him and withdrew his hand,
    using suppliant words, as follows:

7. JOHN: How is it, Lord, that you should be baptized,

cf. Mt 3.14

    for at your Baptism you bring forgiveness to all?
    The Fast looks expectantly towards you;
    sprinkle it with sanctification, and it will be perfected.

8. JESUS: Our Lord spoke: I have willed it,   cf. Mt 3.15
    approach and baptize me, that my will be done.
    Resist my will you cannot;
    I shall be baptized by you, for thus have I willed.

9. JOHN: I beg of you, Lord, let me not be compelled:
    what you ask is hard;
    it is I who need to be baptized by you,   Mt 3.14
    for you, with your hyssop, make all things white.   Ps 51.7

10. JESUS: I have asked, for it has pleased me that it should be so;
    why then, John, do you dispute it?
    Let what right demands be fulfilled;   Mt 3.15
    come, baptize me. Why do you stand there?

11. JOHN: How can mere straw which is like tinder
    grasp fire in its hands?
    O Being of fire, have pity on me,
    let me not come near, it is so hard for me.

12. JESUS: I have revealed to you from the start my will;
    draw near and baptize me, you will not get burnt.
    The bridal chamber is ready, do not hold me back
    from the wedding feast that lies prepared.

13. JOHN: The angels are afraid and do not dare
    to gaze upon you, for fear of being blinded;
    how then can I, Lord, baptize you?
    I am too weak to draw near: please do not reproach me.

14. JESUS: You should be afraid of disputing my will,
    going against what I have asked.
    Baptism awaits me expectantly:
    fulfil the task to which you have been called.

15. JOHN: I proclaimed you by the Jordan   Lk 3.3
    in the hearing of the People who are not easily persuaded;
    if now they see you baptized by me
    they will doubt that you are the Lord.

16. JESUS: I will be baptized while they look on,
    for the Father who sent me will testify
    that I am his Son in whom he is well pleased.

                                                    Mt 3.7 and par.
    He will bring reconciliation to Adam who had earned his
        wrath.

17. JOHN: It is proper, Lord, that I should recognize my true
        nature,
    seeing that I am fashioned out of earth,   Gen 3.19
    whereas you are the fashioner, who gives shape to all.
    How can I baptize you in the water?

18. JESUS: It is proper that you should know why I have come
    and for what reason I have requested you to baptize me:
    this is the middle point of the path I have trod;
    let Baptism not be withheld.

19. JOHN: The river you have come to is too small
    for you to stay there and it contain you:

heaven cannot suffice for your might,
so how can the water of Baptism hold you?

20. JESUS: The womb is yet smaller than the Jordan,
yet of my own will I dwelt in the Virgin.
Just as I was born from the womb,
so shall I be baptized in the Jordan.

21. JOHN: The heavenly hosts stand by,
serried ranks of angels, in worship:
if I should approach to baptize you
I shall quake with fright.

22. JESUS: These crowds of heavenly powers
consider you blessed for baptizing me.
It was for this that I chose you from the womb: Lk 1.41
have no fear, for I have so willed it.

23. JOHN: I have prepared the way for which I was sent,
I betrothed the Bride as I was bidden.   cf. Mt 3.10 and par.
Let your Epiphany increase in the world
now that you are come; but I will not baptize you.

24. JESUS: This is the very preparation I have wished for
—that I should go down and be baptized in the water,
forging armour for those to be baptized,
that they may look upon me and not be vanquished.

Jn 3.14–15 (Num 21.8)

25. JOHN: Why should I baptize the Child of the Father,
seeing that you are in your Father and he in you.
you give sanctification to priests,
so why are you asking for ordinary water?

26. JESUS: The children of Adam are looking to me
to give them new birth:
I shall tread out in the waters a path for them,
and, unless I am baptized, this cannot be done.

27. JOHN: Pontiffs are sanctified by you,
by your hyssop priests are made white;
you create anointed kings,
so how can Baptism benefit you?

28. JESUS: The Bride whom you betrothed to me is expecting
me to go down to Baptism, and then I shall sanctify her.
O friend of the Bridegroom, please do not refuse   Jn 3.29
this washing which is awaiting me.

29. JOHN: I cannot, for I am too weak,
hold in my hands your flame.
Your legions are made of fire:
tell one of the angels to give Baptism to you.

30. JESUS: It is not from the angels that my body was taken,
otherwise I might have called an angel to baptize me.
No, it is Adam's body with which I am clothed,
and you, a child of Adam, shall baptize me.

31. JOHN: The waters saw you and greatly feared,   Ps 77.16
the waters have seen you and are trembling,
the very river bank has shaken with fright.
Why should I, so frail, give you Baptism?

32. JESUS: The waters will be sanctified at my Baptism,
fire and spirit will they receive from me;
unless I am baptized they will not fulfil their proper role
of bearing as fruit immortal offspring.

33. JOHN: If fire should approach your Fire
     it will get burnt up like tinder.
     Mount Sinai could not endure you,
     so how can I in my frailty baptize you?

34. JESUS: I am indeed burning fire,
     but for the sake of humanity I became a child
     in a novel womb—a virgin's,
     and now I am baptized in the Jordan.

35. JOHN: It would be much best if you baptized me,
     for you possess the sanctification that can purify all:
     by you are the unclean made holy.
     Why then should you, who are holy, come to Baptism?

36. JESUS: It would be most appropriate if you gave me Baptism,
     just as I say, without contradicting:
     I baptized you in the womb,   Lk 1.41
     so do you baptize me in the Jordan.

37. JOHN: I am but a weak servant,
     have pity on me, seeing that you give freedom to all.
     I could not even undo your shoe-straps: Mt 3.11 and par.
     whoever is it has made me worthy of your exalted head?

38. JESUS: Servants will receive freedom at my Baptism,
     debts are wiped out when I wash,
     liberty will receive its seal in the water.
     But if I am not baptized, it is all in vain.

39. JOHN: The very air is carrying a garment of light
     in readiness for you, above the Jordan;
     so if it is agreed and you wish to be baptized,
     baptize yourself and accomplish all.

40. JESUS: It is proper that you should baptize me
    lest any go astray and say of me,
    "If he is not someone apart, from the Father's house,
    why is it the Levite is afraid to baptize him?"

41. JOHN: How then, as you are being baptized,
    can I seal prayer by the Jordan,
    since in you are to be seen both Father and Spirit:
    whom, then, as a priest, can I invoke?

42. JESUS: Prayer can be sealed in silence:
    just come and place your hand on me.
    The Father will cry out, in place of a priest,   Mt 3.17 and par.
    whatever is appropriate concerning his Son.

43. JOHN: All the guests who are standing here,
    invited by you, the Groom, will bear witness
    that each day I announced in their midst,
    I am the voice, and not the Word.   Jn 1.20, 23

44. JESUS: O Voice crying in the wilderness,   Is 40.3; Mt 3.3
    perform the task for which you came,
    so that the wilderness, to which you set out,
    may thunder at the prosperity you have proclaimed.

45. JOHN: The commotion of angels has reached my ears:
    from the Father's house I can hear
    the heavenly powers shout out:
    "At your Epiphany, O Groom, both worlds have received life."

46. JESUS: Time presses and the guests are awaiting me
    to see what will happen.
    Come, baptize me, that they may give praise
    to the voice of the Father when it is heard.

47. JOHN: I will obey, Lord, and do as you say.
    Come, then, to Baptism, since your love has so urged you:
    dust gives you worship—to what heights has it come
    that it should place a hand on its Maker!

48. The serried ranks stood in stillness
    as the Bridegroom descended into the Jordan;
    the Holy One was baptized and straightway came up,

                                                        Mt 3.16 and par.

    the light from him shining out into both worlds.

49. The gates of heaven were flung open on high
    as the Father's voice made itself heard:
    "Here is my Beloved, in whom I am pleased;   Mt 3.17 and par.
    come, all you peoples, and worship him."

50. In amazement the onlookers stood there
    as the Spirit came down to witness to him.
    Thanks be to your Epiphany, O Lord, who give joy to all,
    for at your appearance both worlds are illumined.

7. The Sinful Woman who anointed Christ (Luke 7): Ephrem, narrative poem

Introduction

The Sinful Woman who anointed the feet of Jesus in Luke 7.36–50 caught the imagination of many Syriac writers. Unlike the tradition widespread in the medieval West, she was not normally identified as Mary Magdalene (on the basis of a similar episode described in John 12.3); instead she is left anonymous, and it is always the Lukan passage that the Syriac homilists and liturgical poets use. The present narrative poem is attributed to Ephrem, and it is probable that in its original form it does go back to him; the two surviving manuscripts, however, differ in many places, and the one followed here is considerably longer than the other. This will in part be due to later expansion, and it will be noticed that there are some awkward transitions at certain points in the story.

The poem introduces two characters who are absent from the Gospel account, the perfume seller from whom the woman buys the expensive unguent, and Satan who disguises himself as a former lover. It was by way of a Greek adaptation of the poem that the motif of the perfume seller reached the medieval West where it features in some of the miracle plays. At the end of the narrative the text translated here gives a surprising twist to Jesus' words in Luke 7.41–42 to Simeon (who is identified as the Pharisee who had invited Jesus): *he is* the one who owes the most, having failed to show the love for Jesus that she had manifested. This is made possible by a subtle alteration to the wording of Jesus' question: instead of "Which of them will love the creditor the more?" the poem has "Which of them *ought* to love him the more?"

In his writings Ephrem shows a great sympathy for biblical women, and he frequently goes out of his way to put them in a good light.

Translation

Listen and take heart, my beloved,
how God is compassionate:
He forgave the Sinful Woman her sins
and supported her in her grief;
he opened the eyes of the man blind from the womb,

                                                Jn 9.6   5

and the pupils of his eyes beheld the light;
to the paralytic he granted recovery—
he stood up and carried his bed as he walked!   Mt 9.2
—while to us, he has given us Pearls,
his holy Body and Blood.   10
He carried his medicines secretly
but was healing with them openly;
he went about the land of Judah
like a doctor carrying his medicines.
Simeon invited him to a meal,   Lk 7.36,40 15
to eat food in his house.
The Sinful Woman rejoiced when she heard
that he was in Simeon's house, reclining and being entertained.
Her thoughts gathered, like the sea,
and her love seethed like the waves.   20
She saw how the Sea of Mercy
had contained himself in a single place,
so she decided to go and drown
all her wickedness in his waves.
She bound her heart, because it had done wrong,   25
with chains of tears and suffering;
she began to weep to herself,
saying as follows,
"What good to me is this prostitution,
what good is this licentious life?   30
I have made modest people licentious, and not been ashamed,

I have plundered orphans, and felt no fear;
I have snatched away the wares of merchants,
yet my avarice has not had its fill.
I have been like a bow in battle   35
and slain both good and bad;
I have been like a storm at sea,
sinking a boat loaded with many passengers.
Why is it I have not acquired just a single husband
who could rebuke my licentious ways?   40
For a single husband is something from God,
whereas to have many is the work of Satan."
These things did she say in secret,
but she began to act quite openly:
she washed her face and removed from her eyes   45
the eye paint which blinds its beholders;
tears flowed gently from her eyes
on that kohl that had slain many a lover.
She drew off from her hands
the alluring bangles of her childishness;   50
she held them up towards the height
in the direction of the One who knows hidden things.
She stripped off and removed from her body
the fine linen clothes of her prostitute's trade.
She decided to go and put on   55
a lowly garment of suffering;
she drew off from her feet and threw away
her elegant but wanton shoes.
She directed her footsteps
straight for the path to that Heavenly Eagle.   60
She took her gold in the palm of her hand
and raised it up towards the height;
she began groaning out in secret
to him who hears openly,
"This, Lord, is what has come to me from my wicked ways,   65

with it will I acquire salvation;
this money that has been gathered from orphans,
with it will I acquire the Father of orphans."
This is what she said in secret,
but she began to act in the open: 70
she took her gold pieces in one hand
and the alabaster jar in the other;   Lk 7.37
she turned round to go off in haste
to the seller of unguents, all sorrowful.
The seller of unguents saw her and was amazed,   75
he fell into argument with her
and began to say thus
to the harlot at the opening of his words:
"Was it not enough for you, harlot,
to corrupt our whole town?   80
What is the meaning of this garb
that you are sporting today for your lovers?
You have taken off your wantonness
and put on humility.
Previously when you came to me   85
your appearance was quite different from now:
you wore fine clothes
but carried little in the way of gold coins,
yet you wanted the finest unguents
to scent your wanton self;   90
whereas here you are today in shabby attire,
but carrying a huge quantity of gold coins!
I do not understand your change
or why you are wearing these clothes.
Either wear clothes appropriate to the quality of the scent,   95
or buy a cheaper scent that suits your present clothes,
for this scent is neither appropriate or right
for these garments which you are wearing.
Has some merchant met you

who is possessed of great wealth? 100
And have you realized that he does not like
your wanton attire?
Have you stripped off this wanton dress
and put on something modest
so that by wearing all sorts of fashions 105
you can capture all of his wealth?
But if he really likes
this attire, being an upright man,
then alas for him, what has he met with
but a pit that will swallow up all his merchandise! 110
Now I would advise you,
being someone concerned for your advantage,
to give up your many men:
they have not benefited you, ever since you were a child.
Get yourself a single husband 115
who will put a check to your wanton behaviour."
This is what the seller of unguents said,
in his discernment, to the prostitute.
The prostitute then replied
in response to the unguent-seller's words: 120
"Do not admonish me with your talk;
do not foil my purpose with your argument.
I asked for unguent–and I'm not asking for it for nothing:
I have no desire to beat down the price.
Take the gold coins, as much as you want, 125
but give me the very best unguent.
Take something that does not last,
and give me something that does.
I am off to him who is everlasting,
and I will buy something that lasts. 130
As for what you said about a merchant,
it is true that one man has met me today
who carries with him great wealth;

he has stolen me—and I have stolen him:
He has stolen away my wrongdoings and sins,   135
whereas I have stolen his merchandise!
As for what you said to me about a husband,
I have acquired a Husband on high
whose authority endures for ever,
whose kingdom will never come to an end."   140
So she received the oil and set off,
hastening as she went.
But Satan saw her and felt downcast:
he was greatly grieved in his mind.
At one moment he was glad,   145
but at another he was grieved:
because she was carrying the unguent-seller's oil
he was rejoicing in his mind,
but because she was wearing shabby attire
this action of hers caused him fright.   150
He followed her closely,
like a robber trailing a merchant;
he watched her eyes
to see where her gaze was directed;
he kept his eyes on her lips   155
so that he might hear what she was saying.
He came and he went, following her feet
wherever her footsteps directed her.
For Satan has to be very cunning
since he does not know what is hidden.   160
That is why our Lord instructed us
not to raise our voices in prayer,   cf. Mt 6.5–7
lest Satan hear what we are saying
and draw near to oppose us.
Once Satan saw that   165
he could not alter her mind,
he changed his shape

and put on human form;
he took a bunch of young men
resembling her lovers of old.   170
He went and stood in front of her in the road
and began to speak as follows:
"By your life, my woman, tell me,
whither are your footsteps directed?
What is all this haste?   175
You are much more in a hurry than usual.
And what is the meaning of this mean garb?
You've abased yourself to look like a serving girl;
instead of your usual fine linen,
here you are wearing shabby garments!   180
Instead of smart shoes on your feet
you are not even wearing old sandals.
Instead of gold on your hands and feet
you are not even wearing a necklace round your neck.
Instead of your bangles of silver and gold   185
you do not even have any rings on your fingers.
Reveal to me, what is all this that you are after?
I do not understand your change:
has one of your lovers gone and died,
and are you off to bury him today?   190
Let us come along and join you in the funeral procession,
and we will carry, with you, some of the sorrow."
The Sinful Woman answered and said
to the Evil One in reply to his words:
"You have done well to liken me   195
to someone who is going to bury the dead:
the sin of my thoughts has died,
and I am off to bury it."
Satan said in reply
to the sinful woman's words: 200
"Come, woman, let me tell you,

I am a former lover of yours;
I won't be like you;
I will not forsake you.
I will give you once more   205
even more gold than before."
The Sinful Woman said in reply
to Satan, following his words:
"I've been widowed as far as you are concerned, sir;
you are no longer my lover,   210
for I have acquired a Husband on high
who is God above all,
whose authority lasts for ever,
in a kingdom that never comes to an end.
In your presence I say it   215
and repeat it again, without lying:
I was your maidservant, Satan,
from my youth up until now.
I was the bridge for him, upon which he trod,
and I corrupted thousands of men.   220
He applied eye-black and blinded my eyes,
and in my blindness I made many others blind.
I was blind, and was not aware
that there exists One who gives sight to the blind,
but now I am off to get sight for my eyes,   225
and with that light I will bring light to many.
I was a broken woman, but I did not know
that there exists One who bandages up the broken,
but now I am off to bandage up my broken state,
and once I am bandaged, I will do the same for many
     others.   230
I was in bondage, and was unaware
that there exists One who releases those who are bound,
but now I am off to loose my own bonds,
and once I am released I will release many others."

This is what the prostitute said   235
to Satan in her discernment.
He gave a groan in his anguish and wept;
with a wail he said as follows:
"I am defeated by you, woman,
what to do I do not know."   240
Once Satan had seen for himself
that he could not alter her purpose
he began to weep for himself
saying as follows:
"The object of my boasting is now lost,   245
the pride of all my days!
How can I lay for her a snare
now that she has travelled up on high?
How can I shoot at her an arrow
now that her defensive wall is unshakable?   250
I will go instead to Jesus
since it is to him that she is going;
and I will say to him as follows,
and maybe he will feel disgust at her and not receive her:
'This woman who is coming to you   255
is a woman who is a prostitute;
she is flighty and not of good birth,
she's been wanton ever since she was a child.
She has captivated many people
with her filthy prostitution.   260
Whereas you, sir, are an upright man;
everyone is pressing to catch a glimpse of you,
and should the people see you
speaking with a prostitute
everyone will shun you: 265
no one will greet you.'"
This is what Satan said
to himself, on his own.

Then in turn he thought better of it,
saying as follows: 270
"How can I go into the presence of Jesus,
seeing that hidden secrets are revealed to him?
He knows very well who I am—
he has never done me a good turn.
Maybe he will rebuke me and I will wither away   275
with the result that all my tricks will perish.
Instead I'll go to Simeon,
for hidden matters aren't revealed to him;
in his heart I'll hide a hook
and maybe she'll be caught on it.   280
I'll tell him as follows,
'By your life, Simeon, tell me,
this man who is staying in your house,
is he an upright man
and a friend of people who do good?   285
Or is he a friend of malefactors?
I am a man of wealth,
a man with many possessions,
and I want to invite him, just as you have,
to come and bless my belongings.'"   290
Simeon replied as follows
in response to the Evil One's words:
"Ever since the day I first saw him,
I've never seen any immodesty,
only serenity and peace,   295
humility and decorum.
He heals the sick without payment   Mt 14.35 etc.
and bandages up the infirm for free.
When he goes and stands beside a grave
he calls out and the dead arise!   Jn 11.43   300
Jairus summoned him to revive his daughter,   Lk 8.41–2
confident he would revive her,

and while he was going with him on the way,
he gave healing to a sick woman   Lk 8.43–8
who grabbed hold of the edge of his cloak   305
and surreptitiously gained healing from him:
her illness was a serious one, and miserable—
it left her at once!
He went out into the wilderness and saw people hungry,
shattered by hunger: 310
he made them sit down on the grass   Mt 14.19–20
and gave them a good meal, out of his compassion.
He went to sleep in a boat, since he wanted to,   Lk 8.23–4
and the sea rose up against the disciples,
but he got up and rebuked the storm,   315
and it turned into a great calm.
He caught sight of a widow who was bereaved,   Lk 7.12–5
accompanying her only son to his burial:
on the road to the tomb he resurrected him
and returned him to her, filling her heart with joy.   320
In the case of a man who was dumb and blind   Mt 12.22
he gave him healing just by the sound of his voice.
He cleansed some lepers by his mere word   Lk 17.12–4
and gave strength to a paralytic's limbs.   Mt 8.6, 13
In the case of a blind man who was wretched and miserable
                                              Mk 8.24–5   325
he opened his eyes, and the man saw the light;
and with two others, the moment they besought him
                                              Mt 9.27–8
he opened their eyes.
This is what I've heard
at a distance concerning the repute of this man,   330
and so I invited him to bless my belongings,
and bless all my wealth."
Satan answered and said
to Simeon in response to his words:

"You should not praise someone on the basis of what's gone
    before: 335
wait till you know what his end is like.
The man's still thirsty:
He hasn't yet taken pleasure in any wine!
If he leaves your house
without speaking to a prostitute,   340
then he's an upright man,
and not a friend of evil doers."
This is what Satan said
to Simeon in his cunning.
He moved off and stood at a distance   345
to see what would take place.
The Sinful Woman, full of transgressions,
stood pressing against the door.
She plaited wings for her prayers,
and she said as follows: 350
"O Son of the Good One, who have come down to earth
because of Adam's wickedness,
don't close your door in my face,
for it is you who have summoned me—and here I am, having
    come.
I know that you will not refuse me: 355
open up to me the door of your compassion;
let me enter, Lord, and take refuge in you
from the Evil One and his hosts.
I was a sparrow and a hawk has chased me,
so I fled and have sought refuge in your nest.   360
Let me enter, Lord, and find protection in you
from the Evil One and his troops.
I was a lamb, and a wolf savaged me,
so I fled and took refuge in your fold;
open up to me the door of your compassion,   365
so that Satan may not rejoice over me.

I was a heifer who broke your yoke,
but I have returned to you after many years:
lay down on me the shoulder-piece of your yoke
so that I may enter and work in your vineyard." 370
Thus did she say in a hidden fashion,
and she knocked gently.
The Steward of the house peered out and saw her
and the colour of his face was changed.
He began to say 375
to the prostitute at the start of his words:
"Get away from here, you prostitute,
for this man who is staying in our house
is an upright man,
and all the household are clean-living. 380
Isn't it sufficient for you, prostitute,
that you've corrupted the whole town:
you've made perverts out of decent people—and not been
    ashamed.
You have despoiled orphans, without a single blush;
you've snatched goods from merchants, 385
and your brazenness isn't abashed.
From now on your snare won't get anyone,
your trap won't catch anyone any longer:
for this is an upright man,
and all the household are clean-living." 390
The Sinful Woman answered and said
to Simeon after these words:
"Maybe you are the doorkeeper,
one who knows hidden secrets?
Attend to the meal, 395
and you'll be free from blame.
If He wants me to enter
he will give instructions and I'll enter."
Simeon ran and closed the door.

He went in and stood at a distance;   400
for a long while
he didn't attend to the meal.
But he who knows hidden secrets
beckoned to Simeon and said,
"Come here, Simeon, I have something to say to you.   405
Wasn't there someone standing at the door?
Whoever it is, open and let him come in;
let him receive what he needs, and then go.
If he is hungry for bread,
then the table of life is in your house;   410
if he is thirsty for water,
then there is a blessed fountain in your house;
if he is sick and asking for healing,
then a great physician is here in your house.
Allow sinners to see me,   415
because it was for them that I abased myself.
I shall not ascend to heaven,
to the Shekhina that I left
until I'm carrying the sheep
who got lost from my Father's house,   420
escorting it on my shoulders   Lk 15.5
and taking it up to the height."
Simeon answered and said
in response to his words,
"Sir, this woman who is standing   425
at the door is a prostitute.
She is licentious, and of low birth;
she's been wanton ever since she was a girl.
Whereas you, sir, are an upright man,
and everyone comes running to see you: 430
if people see you
talking with a prostitute,
everyone will shun you,

and no one will greet you."
Jesus answered and said   435
in response to his words,
"Whoever it is, open the door for him
and you will be free from reproach.
Even if his misdeeds are many,
it is without reprehension that I bid you."   440
Simeon approached and opened the door.
He began to say as follows:
"Come on in, prostitute,
to this man who is just like you.
You are invited by him before the right time,   445
and here you are standing, ready to seize the opportunity.
Come on in, and carry out your desire
with this man who is just like you."
The Sinful Woman, full of transgressions,
pushed her way in and stood by Jesus.   450
She wove wings for her prayer,
saying as follows:
"O my eyes, become fountains
whose streams never fail;
today wash the feet   455
which have travelled after sinners.
O hair which has grown long with braids,
from my youth up to today,
weary not from wiping dry
this holy body.   460
The mouth which has kissed shameless men
—yes, shameless and wicked men—
do not be abashed of kissing
the body which forgives debts."
Thus did she say in a hidden manner   465
to him who hears openly,
while Simeon stands at a distance

to see what he would do.
He who knows things that are hidden
beckoned to Simeon and said to him,   470
"Come here, Simeon, I want to say something to you.

                              Lk 7.40

What was in your thoughts
concerning this prostitute?
Was your mind thinking
"I have invited this upright man   475
—and here he is with a prostitute kissing him!
I invited him so that he might bless my belongings,
—and here he is with a loose woman embracing him?"
There was a man, Simeon,
who had two debtors;   Lk 7.41–2   480
one owed five hundred,
the other owed fifty.
When the creditor saw
that the two men had nothing,
the creditor remitted   485
and forgave the debts of them both.
In the case of which of them was it right
that he should be the more grateful?
He who was forgiven five hundred,
or he who was forgiven fifty?"   490
Simeon answered and said as follows
to Jesus in reply to his words:
"He who was forgiven five hundred   Lk 7.43
should be much the most grateful."
Jesus replied and said   495
to Simeon in response to his word,
"It is you who owe five hundred
whereas this woman owes fifty!
I entered your house, Simeon,   Lk 7.44–6
and you did not bring water to wash my feet,   500

whereas she whom you called a prostitute
and dissolute from her youth up
has washed my feet with her tears,
and with her hair she has wiped them.
In very truth I say to you 505
that I will record her in the Gospel.
Go, woman, your transgressions are forgiven,
and all your wrongdoing is wiped out."

8. The Sinful Woman and Satan (Luke 7):
anonymous dialogue poem

Introduction

The unknown author of dialogue between the Sinful Woman and Satan clearly knew Ephrem's narrative poem, and specific mention is made of the perfume seller in stanza 48. It is Ephrem's other character, Satan, however, who now takes the major role. Here Satan no longer impersonates one of her former lovers, but he is now an externalisation, as it were, of one aspect of her inmost thoughts, for the poet's aim is to represent the struggle that was going on in her mind whether or not to abandon her former lifestyle and take the very real risk involved in trying to gatecrash a dinner party given by a leading man of the community, and then causing a commotion by wanting to anoint the feet of one of the guests: her worse self, portrayed as Satan, presents all the reasons why it would be much safer not to take the risk of being thrown out and put to shame and made a laughing stock.

Translation

1. He who forgives debts has come down to earth
    and, as David's son, was clothed in a body.
    His compassion compelled him, his love drove him on,
    and so, Lord of all, he came to birth.

2. The Compassionate Doctor turned aside;
    towards sinners he directed his path,
    displaying humility towards them
    so that they might come to him without fear.

3. The body's wounds he bound up with his mercy,
    the soul's stains he cleansed with his sanctity,
    visiting both living and dead with his love,
    being God, the Lord of all.

4. The blind met him—and received sight,
                              Mk 8.22–5; 10.46–52; Jn 9.1–7
    the paralytic who saw him carried his bed,
                              Mt 9.6; Mk 2.9–12; Lk 5.24–25; Jn 5.9
    the lame leapt about like deer,
    entering with him the Temple.   Mt 11.5, 15.31; Lk 7.22

5. He caught Zacchaeus from the fig tree   Lk 19.2–6
    and Zebedee's sons in the boat;   Mt 4.21–22; Mk 1.19–20
    likewise the Samaritan woman beside the well,   Jn 4.6–30
    and the sinful one from Simeon's house: Lk 7.36–50

6. The Sinful Woman heard the report
    that he was dining in Simeon's house.
    She said in her heart, "I will go along,
    and he will forgive me all that I've done wrong.

7. "I yearn actually to see
   the Son of God who has clothed himself in a body.
   Just as he forgives Zacchaeus his sins,
   so in his grace he will have compassion on me.

8. "If a robber who is apprehended should see the king
   he is not put to death.
   I am guilty of death, but if I behold
   the King of kings, then I won't die."

9. Satan saw and realised
   that she was on the point of repentance.
   In his craftiness he approached her
   and began to speak as follows:

10. SATAN: Tell me, my child, why are you crying?
    Explain and tell me what has happened:
    are your lovers cross with you?
    I will make things up; why should you cry?

11. WOMAN: It is God whom I love,
    for he greatly delights in those who repent;
    but I reject you, and those who love you,
    for you are full of deceit, just like them.

12. SATAN: I only spoke out of love for you:
    you know very well that I love you.
    Now, in return for all the good I have done for you,
    here you are reviling me and my friends.

13. WOMAN: In very truth I have rejected you,
    and I don't want any of your good turns.
    The person whom you hate is fortunate:
    he becomes a friend to the Most High.

14. SATAN: If you listen to my advice
     you won't disturb that gentleman:
     he is sitting with the nobility,
     and if he sees you he may well be angry.

15. WOMAN: I'm not taking your advice
     for you greatly dislike those who repent.
     Up to today I have been with you,
     but from today on it is to Mary's Son that I belong.

16. SATAN: He is God's Son, and if you go in
     he's not going to receive you as you would like to suppose:
     he will hold you in abhorrence because of your deeds,
     and you will be an object of shame when you come back.

17. WOMAN: He is God's Son, and he won't be angry
     because he delights in those who repent.
     He is like his Father, full of compassion,
     and his wish is for sinners to return.

18. SATAN: You will be an object of mockery to all the world:
     he won't forgive you if you go in:
     the measure of your deeds is full to overflowing;
     you are not worthy of any forgiveness.

19. WOMAN: I will be mocked by all the world
     if I listen to what you say.
     His mercy is much greater than the world
     and my sin is a small thing for him to forgive.

20. SATAN: He is a judge who cannot be swayed:
     with a just sentence he will condemn you.
     He won't consent to take any bribes:
     if you go in, you will be condemned.

21. WOMAN: He is indeed a judge, but one full of compassion:
    for sinners his door is still open.
    Whether I live or am about to die,
    I will go to kiss his feet this very same day.

22. SATAN: He is holy, and you are unclean;
    with the breath of his mouth he will finish you off.
    You are entirely befouled by sin,
    so why are you going to this holy man?

23. WOMAN: He is indeed holy and pure,
    there is nothing evil abiding in him.
    It is precisely because I am unclean that I'm going
    to this holy man, so that he will make me holy too.

24. SATAN: Woe to you, my girl, if you go:
    he's not going to receive you as you'd like to suppose;
    he's got twelve disciples
    who will all threaten to kill you.

25. WOMAN: All woe is what you deserve
    seeing that you so hate those who repent.
    Those twelve disciples of his
    will supplicate their Master on my behalf.

26. SATAN: You are a prostitute, if only you'd recognize it:
    it is not some dissolute man that you are approaching.
    You're quite out of your mind, girl,
    you don't realize to whom you are going.

27. WOMAN: A prostitute I am—I don't deny it—
    a sister of Rahab who was put on the right path: Josh 2
    it was Joshua son of Nun who saved her,
    Jesus our Lord will save me.

28. SATAN: I can see that you've gone out of your mind,
    you don't know what you are saying.
    You've never read the Scriptures,
    and yet here you are expounding their words!

29. WOMAN: I can see that you are ashamed,
    for the Son of God has condemned you.
    Up to today I belonged to you,
    but from now on I reject you and your friends.

30. SATAN: You'd be better off, my girl, if you stayed back
    and didn't go off to Mary's son.
    Perhaps, unbeknown to you, he's already scowling at you,
    and if he sees you he will be angry.

31. WOMAN: What could be happier than today
    if I go and approach Mary's Son?
    I'd be better off even if he killed me,
    for I'd escape from you, the enemy of everyone.

32. SATAN: My pretty dove, what's up with you?
    Who has wheedled you so that you are rebelling against me:
    It's a long time that you've been living with me;
    are you going to take off, while I look on?

33. WOMAN: I am a guileless dove,
    and I have escaped your claws:
    Christ the Eagle has rescued me,
    and I will live under his wings.

34. SATAN: You are brazen and impudent;
    only the debauched love you.
    You are just an unclean corpse,
    so why are you off to this holy man?

35. WOMAN: I am indeed brazen and impudent,
    and debauched men have loved me,
    but Christ the Bridegroom has betrothed me,
    and he has made me holy, to be with himself.

36. SATAN: You used to go out into the streets every day
    and enslave men by compulsion;
    you've got innumerable lovers:
    you shouldn't be going to Mary's son.

37. WOMAN: Yes, I went out into the streets every day,
    but today I'm off to Simeon's house.
    I loathe you and your friends:
    it is only Jesus whom I love.

38. SATAN: I am your master, and you're enslaved to me:
    why have you rebelled?
    You've been in service for a long time with me,
    and though I've no hate for you, you now hate me.

39. WOMAN: My master you were, but I have broken away:
    woe to those who are in service to you.
    I am now a servant to God's Son:
    His yoke is light for those who repent.   cf. Mt 11.30

40. SATAN: News has gone out to all the world
    of the mark of wrath that is placed upon you.
    No one else who is unclean like you
    will ever dare to draw near to him again.

41. WOMAN: The news has gone out to all the world
    that the Son of God has forgiven my sins;
    for sinners can approach without any fear
    the very day that they repent.

42. SATAN: Your hair, which was scented daily
    with the finest fragrant oil,
    is now, I can see, full of dust,
    like someone who has just buried an only child.

43. WOMAN: My hair was indeed scented every day,
    and with its beauty it ensnared many a man;
    but today I'm sprinkling it with dust,
    ensnaring myself with it.

44. SATAN: Your eyes were made up with eye-black
    and people would be amazed at your beauty,
    but today I see tears
    gushing forth without a stop.

45. WOMAN: My eyes indeed served as traps
    which would ensnare the innocent;
    now they convey a bribe to him
    who is full of mercy, so that he may forgive them.

46. SATAN: Your tongue used to sing every day
    and people would admire in the streets;
    now I see it is full of suffering
    and it resounds with prayers.

47. WOMAN: It is right that the tongue which sang every day
    should now be filled with lament:
    instead of its former laughter,
    it should sing praise to God Most High.

48. SATAN: Why did you go to that seller of perfumes?
    What is that jar for?
    Have your lovers come to visit you?
    Are you wanting to have a fine time with them?

49. WOMAN: It is to God that I am off,
    and I'm taking with me this jar
    in order to anoint that head of life:　　　　Mt 26.7; Mk 14.3
    He will then forgive me my sins, and I will return.

50. SATAN: Your neck, fair lady, you used to adorn
    with necklaces of gold and emerald,
    but today you resemble a widow
    without even the plainest of necklaces.

51. WOMAN: The neck that was daily adorned
    should today be bowed,
    ready to go off to worship the Most High,
    for he will forgive me all that I've done wrong.

52. SATAN: Height and depth and all that they contain
    will be witness at that time
    that he will not receive you if you go in,
    and you'll be an object of shame when you return.

53. WOMAN: Height and depth and all they contain
    will indeed be witness at that time
    that if I go he will receive me
    and will forgive my sins, and then I'll return.

54. SATAN: Heaven and earth will weep for you
    since you have not listened to what I've told you:
    You will go and come back all ashamed.
    What's it to me if I'm not listened to?

55. WOMAN: Heaven and earth will weep for me
    if I listen to what you are urging.
    My hope is with the Lord.
    I am off, and will return rejoicing.

56. SATAN: It will be amazing if he is won over
    and receives you as you imagine;
    yes, truly astonishing, if he opens up a door
    before you, a Sinful Woman.

57. WOMAN: A great door is opened for all,
    and he wills that sinners should repent.
    For he who forgives sins has come down to earth,
    and in those who repent he rejoices and exults.

58. She took the unguent in the jar
    and set off lovingly to God.
    She entered his presence all in tears,
    she received what she wanted, and returned in joy.

59. O Son of God, who opened your mouth
    and forgave the Sinful Woman her sins,
    forgive us our sins too, just as you did her,
    for we have sinned just as she did.

60. And as the Sinful Woman was forgiven
    because she kissed your feet in Simeon's house,   Lk 7.38
    do you forgive your Church
    which, at the altar, consumes your Body and Blood.

9. Two thieves (Luke 23.39–41): anonymous dialogue poem

Introduction

Although the Gospels all refer to the two thieves crucified with Jesus, and the Synoptic ones specify that one was on the left and the other on the right, it is only Luke who has the dialogue between them. Later tradition (followed here) identified the Good Thief as being on the right and the Bad on the left, and (from the sixth century onwards) they were even provided with names, Dumachus and Titus (the exact forms vary). As in a number of other Syriac dialogue poems involving biblical characters, the underlying argument is between a position based on the seemingly clear evidence of external circumstances, and one that recognizes that behind the outward circumstances there is some superior hidden reality.

Translation

1. There fell on my ears the sound of the two thieves
    disputing on Golgotha:
    let us listen, my brothers, to what they are saying
    as they stand in this wondrous judgement court.

2. Between them is our Lord's cross
    acting as the Judge who cannot be swayed:
    like the scales of truth, it weighed out their words
    as they set out their cases.

3. It is written that he was numbered with the wicked,

    Is 53.12; Mk 15.28

    and between two thieves they fixed his cross;

    Mt 27.38; Lk 23.32

while they, erect on their crosses,
disputed over him as they gazed upon him.

4. The thief on the right wore a crown,
    making petition to his Lord:
    he perceived his hidden power
    and so supplicated and asked for mercy.

5. "Remember me, Lord, on the day   Lk 23.42
    you come to the kingdom which passes not away,"
    cried the thief to the Lord of all,
    "Let me behold your compassion that cannot be measured."

6. His companion on the left, who was crucified with him,
    on hearing his words, said,
    "If this man has a kingdom,
    then why does he straddle the shameful cross?"

7. GOOD THIEF: If he had wished it, he would not have been
        crucified:
    He is a hidden King who has entered in
    and I have sought from him mercy once he is revealed
    in great glory—may he have mercy on me!

8. BAD THIEF: Don't you see his body's sufferings,
    how like us, he is pierced with nails?
    If he has a kingdom that he can grant,
    then let him release himself and we will believe him.

                                                cf. Lk 23.39

9. GOOD THIEF: Don't you see how the sun has darkened,
        don't you notice how its light is gone?   Mt 27.45
    Your mind is blinded,
    and you cannot see the King who has been proclaimed.

10. BAD THIEF: He is a man like you, impaled on the wood,
    and his sufferings are even greater than ours.
    If he was a king as you claim,
    he would have gathered his legions to avoid this ignominy.

    cf. Mt 26.53

11. GOOD THIEF: Is he a man when Sheol falls at his cry
    and the earth shakes at his tread? Mt 27.51
    Instead of legions, creation itself has cried out
    that he is a King who cannot be destroyed.

12. BAD THIEF: It is astounding on your part that you do not
        see
    the flail marks all over his back,
    yet here you are proclaiming that it is glory that he possesses!
    Who will believe what you are saying today?

13. GOOD THIEF: It is folly on your part that you do not notice
    how the departed, in groups, clap their hands, Mt 27.52
    leaving their place to go out to meet him.
    But your heart is hardened, and you do not give your assent.

14. BAD THIEF: This king of yours in whom you believe,
    what is his country over which he rules?
    And why is he thus left abandoned and reviled
    if he is indeed a king, as you say?

15. GOOD THIEF: He is King of all worlds, his authority
    is extended everywhere and is indissoluble.
    And I supplicate him to have mercy on me
    in that kingdom which passes not away.

16. BAD THIEF: Then your goal, which you speak of, is Paradise,
    as he has assured you,

but how can someone carrying a cross enter
the Eden to which you are looking?

17. GOOD THIEF: Your goal, to judge by your words, is to be
with the crucifiers, seeing that you are contentious:
those men on the left, whose leader you are,
beheld mighty acts, but failed to believe.

18. BAD THIEF: Crushed by anguish and burdened with pain,

Is 53.3

vinegar is mixed for him and his side is pierced.

Mt 27.48; Jn 19.34

He is filled with all manner of sufferings:
how can I call him king, as you say?

19. GOOD THIEF: Creation has been shaken, do you not shake
too?　　　　　　　　　　　　　　　Mt 27.51
The elements have reeled, do you not reel too?
Rocks are rent, and do you still deny?
Confess and live; why are you so stubborn?

20. BAD THIEF: We were companions in crime;
when you have become a child of that kingdom, as you claim,
then the blood of the murdered will groan out against you,

Gen 4.10

and you will not be held worthy of that kingdom.

21. GOOD THIEF: I am indeed your companion, but because I
have believed
the Crucified One makes a distinction between you and me:
He has sprinkled his blood on me and I have been cleansed;
he promised me love—and I fully believed him.

22. BAD THIEF: You are wrong, my friend, don't be so confident
that a crucified man can bring you

into that kingdom which does not pass away:
if he really could, he would never have been crucified.

23. GOOD THIEF: You are wrong, and do not lead me astray:
there is no way I can be wrong, so why be so importunate?
I have as a key the word of my Lord:
with it I will open up and enter the Garden of Eden.

24. BAD THIEF: Jesus is just an ordinary man, crucified with us:
had he been able to, he would have saved himself.
Here he is fettered, so how can he possibly
invite you to Eden, as you have said?

25. GOOD THIEF: Jesus rides the wooden cross below,
but on high his chariot is harnessed in readiness.   Ezek 1
He is Lord of Nature, which has recognized him:
and Nature is stunned because he is crucified.

26. BAD THIEF: A crown of thorns is set on his head,
                                                    Mt 27.29; Jn 19.2
his side is pierced and he is filled with suffering.   Jn 19.34
What king is there in such a state,
abused, and abandoned by his soldiers?

27. GOOD THIEF: This man's crown cannot be seen
except by the soul that discerns:
if only you would turn your gaze upwards,
then you would see his diadem that never decays.

28. BAD THIEF: When did this happen to any king,
that a crown of thorns was placed on his head?
When and where have you ever heard
that such a diadem should belong to a king?

29. GOOD THIEF: This is something no man can do:
    only Jesus, who is King of all,
    for with his thorns he has torn out earth's thorns,
    so that Adam might escape from that curse.   Gen 3.18

30. BAD THIEF: He is quite dead now, having drunk death's cup,
    if only you would look.
    He will spend the night in Sheol, so why go on insisting
    that you will be with him in the Garden of Eden?

31. GOOD THIEF: This man's death has uprooted Sheol:
    He will empty that well-fed place.
    His cry has overthrown it, and Sheol no longer stands:
                                                        Mt 27.50
    for this reason is he entering it—so as to empty it!

32. BAD THIEF: Let us listen now to what the scribes of the
        people have to say,
    how they are jeering!   Mt 27.41
    Everyone is shaking their head at him,   Mt 27.39
    and it is only you who have confessed him.

33. GOOD THIEF: Let us listen instead, if only you would
        attend,
    to the sound of the rocks that are splitting
    and the bones of the dead that are gathering together.
                                                        Ezek 37
    Why is it, my friend, that you do not believe?

34. BAD THIEF: I have taken a good look at him,
    but have seen in him no sign of glory, such as you said.
    All sorts of dishonours are visible there,
    but where is the glory which you are proclaiming?

35. GOOD THIEF: Many things, if only you look for them,
    point to how glorious he is:
    His very creation testifies to him,
    seeing that it all trembles at his sufferings.

36. BAD THIEF: He entered the court room and was flogged
    along with us,   Mt 27.26
    and in the sentence, he is crucified with us too.
    Pilate has given sentence and condemned him:
    had he been a king, Pilate would never have handed him over.

37. GOOD THIEF: In the accusation that is written above him
    Pilate himself calls him King: Jn 19.19
    are you disputing with the scribes who cried out
    in witness to the fact that he had described him as King?

38. BAD THIEF: His entire body is stripped and laid bare,
    his feet and his hands are pierced;
    he endures tremors, yet still you dispute
    about that kingdom which he does not have!

39. GOOD THIEF: There is a great gulf now between you and
    me:
    the Crucified One acts as the boundary which you cannot
    cross.
    Take your place on the left,
    for the right hand is mine, since I have believed.

40. BAD THIEF: The people who judged and condemned him
    have crucified him:
    his cross testifies that he is stretched out with us.
    Let him save himself, along with me and you.   Mt 27.40
    Then I will believe in accordance with what you are saying.

41. GOOD THIEF: His cross shatters the gates of Sheol,

Mt 16.18

    the sun has darkened, and the universe shakes;
    the Temple curtain he has rent in two: Mt 27.51
    all this testifies that he is Lord of all.

42. BAD THIEF: I heard his voice crying out in complaint
    in the midst of his sufferings when he gave up his spirit.
    I do not believe that, if he had been able,
    he would have remained on the cross in the way you have
        said.

43. GOOD THIEF: How is it you do not hear the earthquake's
        sound,
    and the cry of creation as all things complain?
    The very world's foundations are shaking,
    stunned at hearing his cry.

44. BAD THIEF: Cannot you hear the tumult among the people,
    how they are saying just what I am saying,
    that if he is truly the Son of God,   Lk 23.35
    let him revive himself and we will believe in him.

45. GOOD THIEF: Listen, friend, to the tumult among the dead
    who have come out from their own place:
    look at this Jesus in whom I believe—
    he is reviving the dead, just as I have proclaimed.

46. BAD THIEF: That king in whom you have believed has gone
        to his repose.
    Who will now bring you into the Garden?
    Why did he not take you and fly off on high
    if he had to power to do so, as you have said?

47. GOOD THIEF: He is gone to his repose so as to wake up
      dead Adam:
    those who are reposing in Sheol are looking out for him.
    He is untying Adam who had been bound,
    and as for me, he will bring me to that Garden of Eden.

48. BAD THIEF: I am quite amazed that you should believe
    in a man put to death, who is now dead and gone.
    Who would be attracted by what you have said,
    apart from you who have fallen in love with him!

49. GOOD THIEF: I am quite amazed that you still blaspheme
      against the Son of God
    who died of his own volition.
    Let your mouth be silent, for it is full of offence.
    Blessed is the Crucified One whom I have confessed.

50. Blessed is the Crucified One who judged and condemned
    the thief on the left who blasphemed against him,
    while to the thief on the right, who asked for mercy,
    he promised that place which is filled with life.

51. Well did he promise to the thief who believed him
    that he would be with him in the Garden of Eden.   Lk 23.43
    In your kingdom, Lord, have mercy on me,   Lk 23.42
    and may I who have confessed you see your compassion too.

10. The Cherub and Thief (Luke 23.43):
anonymous dialogue poem

Introduction

Christ's words to the penitent thief crucified beside him, that "this day you will be with me in Paradise" (Luke 23.43), implicitly point the reader back to the Paradise narrative in Genesis where, after Adam and Eve's disobedience and their banishment from Paradise, the entry to Paradise is barred by a Cherub with a flaming revolving sword (Gen 3.24; the Syriac translation has the singular Cherub, whereas the Hebrew and hence modern translations have the plural, Cherubim). Since the Cherub had been ordered not to let human beings back into Paradise, how then did the penitent thief gain access? This lively poem offers the answer: it is only when the thief finally produces the cross (stanza 41; cf. 5) that the Cherub finally gives way and allows him in.

This has proved to be one of the most popular of the dialogue poems, for there are no less than three different translations of it into Modern Syriac. It is still sometimes acted out in a stylized way, usually on Holy Saturday; a description of this, as observed at the end of the nineteenth century by F. F. Irving in the village of Ula, near Salmas (northwest Iran), reads as follows:

> The priest clothed the deacon in his priestly vestment called
> *Ma'apra*, and gave him also the book of the Gospels and the
> cross. He then returned alone into the sanctuary, dropping
> the veil, and thus excluding himself from view. Then began
> a lengthy dialogue, in musical recitative, between the priest
> and the deacon, in alternate verses; the former personify-
> ing the angel with the flaming sword who kept the Gate of
> Paradise, the latter the repentant thief who had come to seek
> admission on the strength or our Lord's promise. . . . First the
> thief asks admission to Paradise. But the angel replies: "You

are a thief, a murderer, an infidel. Why come you here? This is no place for robbery. Surely you have missed your road?" The thief gives answer: "Truly I *was* a thief, and much ill I did. But I mourned and repented: and by the word of Christ I come here now. For with him I was crucified."

Then after much questioning the angel asks for a sign that Christ has indeed sent him. Thereupon the thief produces the cross, which hitherto has been concealed from sight, and proclaims that this is the key which will open Paradise. The angel thereupon admits his claim, saying: Praise to Thee, O Christ our King, Thou hast forgiven Adam's sin, and opened the way of life to Titus [the traditional name of the penitent thief] by the cross which we adore.

The deacon then enters the Sanctuary, and the service proceeds as usual.

Translation

1. At the Crucifixion I beheld a marvel
    when the thief cried out to our Lord,
    "Remember me, Lord, on the day when you come
    to that kingdom which does not pass away."   Lk 23.43

Refrain: Praise to you, Lord, for at your coming
    sinners turned back from their wickedness;
    they entered and found shelter
    in the Garden of Eden—which is the holy Church.

2. He made a petition, stretched out and gave it
    to the crucified King, asking for mercy;
    and he who is full of mercy heard his cry
    and opened the door to his request.

3. "Remember me, Lord," was what he cried out on the cross,
    "in that kingdom which does not pass away,   Lk 23.43
    and in that glory in which you will be revealed
    may I behold your rest, seeing that I have acknowledged you."
    cf. Lk 12.8

4. Our Lord replied, "Since you have acknowledged me
    this very day you shall be in the Garden of Eden;
    in very truth, man, you will not be kept back
    from that kingdom to which you are looking.

5. "Take with you the cross as a sign, and be off:
    it is a great key whereby the mighty gate
    of that Garden shall be opened,
    and Adam, who has been expelled, shall enter again."
    Gen 3.24

6. The word of our Lord was sealed
    like a royal missive from the palace;
    it was handed over to the thief
    who took it and made off for the Garden of Eden.

7. The Cherub heard him and rushed up,
    he grabbed the thief at the gate,
    stopping him with the sharp blade that he held.
    All astonished, he addressed him as follows:

8. CHERUB: Tell me, my man, who has sent you?
    What is it you want, and how did you get here?
    What is the reason that brought you here?
    Reveal and explain to me who it is who has sent you.

9. THIEF: I will tell you who has sent me,
    just hold back your blade and listen to my words.

I am a thief, but I supplicated for mercy,
and it was your Lord who sent me on my way here.

10. CHERUB: By what powerful means did your arrival take
        place?
    Who brought you to this dread spot?
    Who transported you across the sea of fire
    so that you could enter Eden? Who is it who sent you?

11. THIEF: It was through the power of the Son, who sent me,
    that I crossed over and came here without hindrance.
    Through him I subdued all powers,
    and I have come to enter here, seeing that he has given me
        confidence.

12. CHERUB: You are indeed a thief, just as you have said,
    but you can't steal into this region of ours:
    it is fenced in with the sword that guards it.   Gen 3.24
    Turn back, my man, you have lost your way.

13. THIEF: I was indeed a thief, but I have changed:
    it was not to steal that I have come here.
    Look, I've got with me the key to Eden,
    to open it up and enter: I will not be prevented.

14. CHERUB: Our region is awesome and cannot be trodden,
    for fire is its indomitable wall;
    the blade flashes out all around it.
    How is it you have made so bold as to come here?

15. THIEF: Your region is indeed awesome, just as you have said,
    —but only until our Lord mounted the cross,
    when he transfixed the sword of all suffering
    so that your blade no longer kills.

16. CHERUB: Ever since the time that Adam left
     I haven't ever seen anyone turn up here;
     your race has been banished from the Garden;
     you shall not enter it, so don't argue any more.

17. THIEF: Ever since the time that Adam left
     your Lord has been angered at our race,
     but now he is reconciled and has opened up the gate.

                                                    Eph 2.16

     It is to no purpose that you are standing here.

18. CHERUB: You should realize that it isn't possible
     for an unclean man to enter in here
     —and you are a murderer, and a shedder of blood.
     Who is it who has brought you to this pure place?

19. THIEF: You should realize that such is the wish
     of him who makes the unclean clean, who was crucified
          together with me;
     with the blood from his side he has washed me completely
          clean.   Jn 19.34
     It was he who has sent me to Paradise.

20. CHERUB: Be off with you, man, and don't argue any further,
     for this is what I have been ordered:
     to guard from your race, by means of the sword,
     the Tree of Life that is to be found in here.   Gen 3.22

21. THIEF: Be off with you, angel; you should learn and see
     that I've left behind, hanging on Golgotha,
     that very Fruit of Salvation that's in your garden
     —so that our race may now enter without any hindrance.

22. CHERUB: Eve and Adam fell into debt and wrote out
     a document that will not be erased: Col 2.14

they went out of here under sentence
to live in low estate in the land of thorns.   Gen 3.18

23. THIEF: The debt is repaid. Just listen, O Cherub:
    the document has now been transfixed on the cross;   Col 2.14
    by means of both blood and water your Lord has wiped it out,
    and pinned it there with nails so that it won't be exacted.

24. CHERUB: Adam was driven out from this Garden,
    and there is no way he can enter here again,
    for the sword's blade is revolving,
    and he'll encounter it should he come near.

25. THIEF: He who was driven out has returned to his Father's
        house,
    for the great Shepherd has gone out and found   Jn 10.11
    that sheep that had left the Garden;
    carrying him on his shoulders, he has escorted him back.
                                                          Lk 15.5

26. CHERUB: It is something totally novel that I've seen today:
    a path leading back into the Garden.
    But here are Adam's footprints, take a look:
    he has left here and not returned again.

27. THIEF: Jesus your Lord has performed a novel deed,
    for now he has released Adam who had been confined;
    he has raised up whole crowds from inside Sheol,   Mt 27.52
    and they have sent me in advance, to open up for them.

28. CHERUB: I am the cherub: how is it you have transgressed
    against my office of guarding, with which I've been entrusted?
    A fiery being like me cannot be vanquished,
    but as for you, an offspring of Adam, how bold you are!

29. THIEF: I am your companion and we have but a single Lord
    in common for both of us;
    his authority is much higher than either yours or mine,
    and so I've no fear, seeing that it was he who has sent me.

30. CHERUB: You simply cannot enter in here,
    for it is a resplendent place that no one can tread:
    the Shekhina is escorted around inside it,
    and the sword of fire is guarding it.

31. THIEF: You cannot hold anyone back,
    for the sword is now blunted and made dull.
    The cross has opened up the Garden of Eden;
    there's no means by which it can still be kept closed.

32. CHERUB: Haven't you heard from the Bible
    how the cherub and the sword go round
    guarding the way to the Garden of Eden,   Gen 3.24
    so that none of Adam's offspring can enter here?

33. THIEF: Haven't you heard from the revelation
    that your Lord has come down and become man,
    thus reconciling Adam, who was in a state of anger,
    bringing back to Eden the one who had been driven out?

34. CHERUB: The sign of the revolving sword
    that guards the Tree of Life   Gen 3.22–4
    frightened off Adam when he was driven out,
    so how is it that you're not afraid?

35. THIEF: The sign of your Lord is with me,
    and by it the sharp sword is blunted;
    by it, too, is the sentence remitted,
    and by it, Adam, once expelled, shall return.

36. CHERUB: The ranks of fire are standing here,
      thousands of them in bands innumerable;
      the multitudes are awesome, and quite simply
      you can't travel on any further and enter among them.

37. THIEF: The multitudinous ranks of which you've told me
      are themselves in awe as they look upon the cross:
      the sign of the Son inspires them with awe,
      and they worship before it, while me they hold in honour.

38. CHERUB: The sign of my Lord is upon the Chariot,   Is 66.15
      resplendent upon the Throne, but from us it is hidden,

                                                                    Ezek 1.26–7

      so how is that you—as you are claiming—
      carry this sign of his and escort it?

39. THIEF: His sign is upon the Chariot above,
      but look, his cross is on Golgotha below,
      and with his own blood he has written a new missive
      permitting Adam to come back into the Garden.

40. CHERUB: O agent in blood, who has brought you here?
      Who is it has sent you, a murderer?
      The sword is drawn, and if you make bold
      the blade will flash out against you.

41. THIEF: O agent for the King, don't be upset;
      your authority is repealed, for your Lord has willed it so.
      It is his cross that I've brought to you as a sign:
      look and see if it's genuine, and don't be so angry.

42. CHERUB: This cross of the Son which you've brought to me
      is something I dare not look upon at all.

It is both genuine and awesome; no longer will you be
   debarred
from entering Eden, seeing that he has so willed it.

43. THIEF: The cross of your Lord has breached the fence

Eph 2.14

that had been built up between us and you,
Anger has passed away, and peace has come,
and the path to Eden is no longer cut off.

44. CHERUB: He who was slain has sent to me and testified with
      his own blood
that I should let go of the blade which I've been wielding.
Fearful is this sign which you have brought me;
enter in, O heir; I will not turn you back.

45. THIEF: Resurrection has occurred for the race of humankind
that had been thrust out of their home.
You cherubim and angels, rejoice with us,
for we have returned now to your city.

46. CHERUB: Great is the compassion that has been shown to
      you,
the descendants of Adam who sinned and thus died.
Enter, thief, you will not be kept back,
for the gate is now open for those who repent.

47. THIEF: Great and most glorious is the compassion of my
      Lord,
for his mercy has effected and his love has compelled him.
Rejoice with us, O spiritual beings,
for we have been mingled into your race.

48. CHERUB: The Gentle One has held back from your race
the blade and the sword that I have been wielding.

Outcasts who have returned, have no fear,
enter inside the Garden with exultation.

49. THIEF: Praise be in Eden that is now at peace,
peace on earth which has been liberated.
Blessed is the Crucified One who has reconciled us
so that we shall no longer be deprived of your race.

50. Thanks be to you, O Lord of all,
who have brought back Adam who had been driven out,
while to the thief who asked for mercy
you opened up the gate that had been closed.

51. Thanks be to you, at whose word
the thief entered into the Garden of Eden,
and there was good hope for Adam again,
and he returned to the place from which he had gone out.

11. Death and Satan (Matthew 27.50, 52): Ephrem, Nisibene Hymns, 41

Introduction

The Descent of Christ to Sheol, the abode of the dead, is only alluded to in the New Testament (notably 1 Peter 3.20, especially in the Syriac translation), but it soon became a theme of central importance for Syriac and Eastern Christianity. Whereas the incarnation describes the entry of God the Word into historical time and geographical space, the Descent into Sheol decribes his entry into sacred time and sacred space, thus indicating that the salvation brought about by the incarnation is not limited by the particularity of historical time and geographical place, but is effective at all times and in all places. At the Descent Christ, the Second Adam (cf. 1 Cor. 15.47), is understood as rescuing the First Adam (humanity) from the grip of Death and Satan.

Because the Descent belongs outside human earthly experience, it cannot be described in factual terms, and so Ephrem has to resort to *mythopoeia*, imaginative story telling, when he wishes to indicate what the Descent is all about. He does so by presenting a series of dramatized scenarios where Death and Satan argue over what the death of Jesus might mean for them. In one small group of poems he employs the ancient Mesopotamian genre of precedence dispute, where Death and Satan each claims to have the greater power over human beings. As the following short excerpt indicates, their knowledge of the biblical text is exceptionally good!

DEATH: Take the case of Samuel,
who spurned you in the matter of gold, Satan,   1 Sam 12.1–4
I vanquished this victor
who had won a victory against bribery.   1 Sam 25.1

SATAN: Take Samson who, in the case of the lion's whelp,
despised you, O Death;   Judg 14.15
by means of Delilah—a delightfully easy tool—
I harnessed him to the millstone.   Judg 16.21

DEATH: Josiah from his youth up
despised you, O Evil One,   2 Kg 22.1–2
yet even in his old age
he could not get the better of me.   2 Kg 23.29–30

SATAN: Hezekiah got the better of you, Death,
when he overcame his allotted span of life,   Is 38.5
but I upset him when he abandoned
the due sense of awe and disclosed his treasures. Is 39.4
                         (Nisibene Hymns, 53:18–21)

In a larger number of poems, of which the one translated here is an example, Ephrem offers a variety of more discursive scenarios. The dramatic moment envisaged is the time of Christ's death on the cross. Although this might seem a victory for Satan (here called the "Evil One," as often in Syriac), he is nonetheless wary, in view of the various miracles of reviving the dead which were performed by Christ. Satan's followers try to reassure him with the example of Elisha who died after reviving a child, but this backfires, owing to Satan's better knowledge of the biblical text. Death at first is more confident, gloating over his catch, but by the time Satan comes to take a look at Jesus lying dead in Sheol, he finds Death downcast, since he has just lost a whole lot of the dead, who had arisen at the moment of Jesus' own death (Matthew 27.52). Satan suggests opening Sheol's gate so that they can jeer at Jesus—but they end up groping around like the men of Sodom, being blinded by the radiance from Christ's face.

Translation

1. The Evil One said, "I am afraid
    of this Jesus in case he may wreck my plans.
    Here I am, thousands of years old,
    and I've never had a moment free from activity:
    I've not seen anything in existence that I've neglected or let
        go;
    and now there comes along someone who makes the
        debauched chaste,
    causing me to lament from now on because he is destroying
    all that I've built up. I have labored much in giving
        instruction,
    for I have enshrouded the whole of creation in all kinds of
        evil."

Refrain: Blessed is he who has come and laid bare
    the wiles of the Crafty One.

2.   "I matched my course with the swift,
    and outstripped them; I engaged in battle,
    and the multitudinous throng served as my weapon:
    I rejoiced in the throng of the populace,
    for they gave me a little opportunity, seeing that the impact
    of numbers is powerful. With a huge army
    I raised up a great mountain of a tower, stretching it up to
        heaven.   Gen 11.4
    If they could wage war with the height,
    how much more will they defeat this man who fights on
        earth!

3.   "Using whatever opportunity the occasion offers
    I wage war with discretion.
    The Jewish people heard that God was one,   Deut 6.4
    but they made themselves a multitude of gods;   Jer 2.28
    but when they saw the Son of God,
    they rushed back to the one God, so that on the pretext
    of confessing God, they denied his Son: pretending to show
        zeal,
    they were running away from him—so that on every occasion
    they are found to be perverse, because they are godless.

4.   "I have a great many years' experience,
    and no child have I ever disdained—
    indeed I have been very attentive to children,
    making sure that they acquired bad habits from the very start,
    so that their faults might grow as they themselves grew up.
    There are some stupid fathers
    who do not injure the seed that I have sown in their sons,

while others, like good farmers,
have uprooted those faults from the minds of their children.

5. "Instead of using a chain, I have bound men
with sloth, and they have sat down idle.
Thus I have deprived their senses from doing anything good:
their eyes from reading, their mouth from singing praise,
their minds from learning.
How keen they are for barren and useless tales!
At empty talk they excel.
But should the Word of Life be mentioned in their presence,
either they will drive it out, or get up and leave.

6. "However many Satans there are in a person,
it is I alone whom everyone curses.
A man's anger is like
a devil which harasses him daily. Other demons are like
travellers,
who only move on if they are forced to;
but with anger, even if all the righteous adjure it,
it will not be rooted out from its place.
Instead of hating destructive envy,
everyone hates some weak and wretched devil!

7. "The snake-charmer is put to shame along with the enchanter
who daily brings snakes into submission.
The viper which is inside him defies him,
for he fails to subdue the lust within himself:
hidden sin is like a snake—when it breathes on him,
he gets burnt right up. Even when he has succeeded in
catching the viper,
using his skill, delusion strikes him secretly:
he lulls the serpent with his incantations,

but by these same incantations he arouses against himself
    great wrath.

8. "I set my stings, and sat and waited.
Who else has so stretched out his patience with everyone?
I sat beside the longsuffering, and gradually bewitched him
until he was reduced to despair.
As for the person who shrinks from sin, habit subdued him:
little by little I wore him down,
until he came under my yoke;
once he had come and got used to it,
he did not want to leave it again.

9. "I perceived and saw that the longsuffering person
is someone who can subdue everything. When I conquered
    Adam,
he was only one, so I left him until he had fathered children,

                                          Gen 4.1–2

and I looked for some other work:
so that idleness might have no experience of me,
I started counting the sand of the sea,   Ben Sira 1.2
to make myself patient, and to test my memory to see if it
    could cope
with mankind once they had multiplied;
before they did so, I had tried them in many ways!"

10. The servants of the Evil One disputed with him,
refuting his words with their own rejoinders:
"Look at Elisha who brought a dead man back to life,

                                2 Kg 4.10, 34–5

who overcame death in the upper room, reviving the widow's
    son:
he is now subdued in Sheol." Because the Evil One
was very quick-witted he refuted their words

by means of their own words:
"How can Elisha be defeated, seeing that he has, in Sheol
    itself,
brought back the dead to life by means of his bones?

                                       2 Kg 13.21

11. "If Elisha, who was insignificant,
    had such great power in Sheol
    —if he could raise up one dead man there,
    how many dead will the death of the mighty Jesus raise?
    You should learn from this, my companions,
    how much greater is this Jesus than us,
    seeing that he has cunningly led you astray
    and you failed to take in his greatness,
    merely comparing him to the prophets.

12. "Your consolations are of little help,"
    says the Evil One to his entourage,
    "How can Death contain
    the man who raised up the dead Lazarus?   Jn 11.44
    And if Death does conquer him, it is because he willingly
    subjects himself, and if he willingly subjects himself to it,
    then you should fear him all the more, for he will not die
    to no purpose. He'll be the cause of great grief to us,
    for by dying he will enter in and raise up Adam to life."

13. Death peered out from inside his cavern,
    astonished to see our Lord crucified:
    "Where are you now, raiser of the dead?
    Will you be food for me, in place of the tasty Lazarus Jn 11.44
    whom I still savour in my mouth? Let Jairus' daughter

                                         Lk 8.55

    come and see this cross of yours;
    let the widow's son gaze upon you.   Lk 7.15

A tree caught Adam for me,   Gen 2.17, 3.6
blessed is the cross that caught the son of David for me!"

14. Death opened his mouth and further said,
    "Have you never heard, son of Mary,
    of Moses, how he excelled all men in his greatness,
    how he became a god, performing the works of God,

                                              Ex 4.16, 7.1, 12.29
    by killing the Egyptian firstborn, and saving the Hebrew?
    How he held back the plague from the living?   Num 16.48
    Yet I went up with the same Moses to the mountain,
    and God—blessed be his honour—handed him over to me in
        person.   Ezek 3.12; Deut 34.5
    However great one of Adam's sons becomes, he will return as
        dust to dust, for he comes from the earth."   Gen 3.19; 2.7

15. Satan came along with his soldiers
    to look at our Lord lying in Sheol
    and to rejoice with Death, his fellow counsellor,
    but he saw him all gloomy, and bewailing the dead,
    who, at the Firstborn's cry, had come to life,   Mt 27.50, 52
    and departed from Sheol. The Evil One arose to comfort
        Death,
    his relative, "You have not lost as much as you have gained:
    as long as Jesus is in your grasp,
    everyone who has lived and is living will come into your
        hands.

16. "Open up so that we can see him and jeer at him,
    let us take up the refrain and say, "Where is your power?"
    Three days are already passed;
    let us say to him, "You, who are three days dead,
    raised up Lazarus, four days dead; raise up yourself now!""
    Death duly opened up the gates of Sheol,

and out from it shone the radiance of our Lord's face!
Like the men of Sodom they were all smitten,   Gen 19.11
they groped around looking for Sheol's gate, which had
   disappeared.

12. The risen Christ and Mary (John 20): anonymous dialogue poem

Introduction

The starting point for this dialogue is John 20.15–16, the encounter of Mary with the risen Christ whom she takes to be the gardener. In John's Gospel the Mary in question is Mary Magdalene, but a widespread early Syriac tradition identified the Mary of this episode as Mary the mother of Jesus, and the words "*my* Son" in the second stanza indicate that this is the case in the present poem as well.

Translation

1. On Sunday, in the morning early   Jn 20.1
   along came Mary to the tomb.

2. MARY: Who will show me, she was saying,
   my Son and my Lord for whom I am seeking?

3. As the Gardener did our Lord appear
   to her, answering and speaking to her thus:

4. GARDENER: Disclose to me, O lady, what it is
   you are seeking today in this garden.   Jn 20.15

5. MARY: O Gardener, please do not refuse me,
   do not drive me from your garden.

6. It is a single fruit that is mine;
    apart from it there is nothing else that I seek.

7. GARDENER: At this season you should realize
    that no fruits are to be found in any garden;

8. so how is it that you are telling me
    that you are looking for fruit today?

9. MARY: You should know, O Gardener,
    that the fruit for which I am searching

10. will give me life—such is my hope—
    if I should but happen to see it.

11. GARDENER: What is this fruit, young lady,
    about which you speak such amazing words?

12. MARY: I know very well and am quite certain
    that the sight of it is too exalted for the eye.

13. GARDENER: How you weary me with your talk,
    how you vex me with what you say.

14. MARY: Where have you removed him? Disclose this to me,
    for I am going after him, seeking him.

15. GARDENER: Why, lady, do you seek
    the living in Sheol, the devourer?   Lk 24.5

16. He concerning whom you are asking
    has left the tomb this very night,

17. while the guards were wielding swords,
    resembling raving dogs.

18. MARY: Concerning his resurrection disclose and explain to
        me
    so that I may be believing in him.

19. For he flew down from highest heaven
    and dwelt in a virgin womb.

20. GARDENER: Incline your ear, O lady, and listen,
    so that I may be the one to show you concerning him.

21. His resurrection gives witness to her who bore him,
    his mother gives witness to his resurrection;

22. height and depth are my witnesses
    that, transcending nature, he was both born and now has
        arisen.

23. She heard his voice and recognized him,
    for he repeated the words "Mary, Mary."   Jn 20.16

24. MARY: Come to me, my Lord and my Master,
     for now I forget my anguish.

25. Come in your compassion, O Son of Mary,
    just as you came to Mary;

26. and with you, at your resurrection, let your light shine forth
    on me and on him who composed this.

From Bible to Liturgy

1. Annunciation: anonymous hymn

Introduction

The Syriac poets have a predilection for letter imagery, and in this poem for the Feast of the Annunciation Gabriel is again portrayed as conveying his message in the form of a letter from the Father, addressed to Mary. At first Mary is perplexed and wonders in her mind who this "fiery being" might be. Gabriel reassures her, and repeats his message. Mary then questions him how this can happen seeing that she has no husband (Lk 1.34). As in the Dialogue between the Angel and Mary (Chapter IV, no. 2), it is the mention of the coming of the Holy Spirit upon her which resolves the matter for her.

Translation

1. The Father wrote out a letter
    and sent it, at the hands of a Watcher, to Nazareth,   Lk 1.26
    to a virgin, Mary, in whom he was well pleased and so chose
        her to become
    mother to his Only-Begotten
    when he descended to deliver all worlds.

Refrain: Blessed is that mouth which announced to Mary!

2. From amidst the fiery legions,
    from the thousands and myriads who stand ready,
    from the choirs of fire, the ranks of flame,
    was Gabriel sent
    to the Virgin, to announce that she was to conceive.

3. God gave Gabriel the command
    and he flew down amidst great commotion,
    bearing that letter full of fair tidings,
    to bring peace to those in a state of wrath,
    seeing that reconciliation had taken place between God and
        the world.   cf. Lk 2.14; Col 1.20

4. The messenger learnt the secret
    and fluttered down, arriving at Nazareth.
    As he beheld the Virgin, he bowed down in reverence,
    then stretched out his hand and gave her the letter of peace
    that had been sent from above.

5. "Peace be with you, O daughter of humanity,
    for you have been chosen to become the tabernacle
    to the Lord of Majesty who is coming down from on high
    to visit the depth below
    and to raise Adam up to the Garden.

6. "Salutation to you, who are filled with grace,   Lk 1.28
    my Lord is with you, O palace of the Most High,
    for in you will the King reside, and in you shall the Light
        shine out.
    From you there shall come forth into creation
    that Hero who will deliver the world."

7. The maiden heard this salutation
   from the man of fire who announced it;
   her senses were perturbed, her thoughts were dismayed,
   she stood there in amazement
   and said secretly to herself,

8. "Whence comes this man of fire?
   Why should a spiritual being come to visit me?
   Who is he? To what place does he belong?
   Who is 'his Lord,' that he said to me,   Lk 1.28
   'My Lord is with you'? He has upset and perturbed me."

9. The Watcher spoke to the maiden,
   "Do not be upset, Mary; salutation to you,   Lk 1.30
   for you shall conceive and give birth to the Wonderful; Is 9.6
   from your womb the Sun shall shine forth   Mal 4.2
   and he will drive out the world's darkness."

10. Mary says to the angel,   Lk 1.34
    "Explain to me, O fiery being, what you mean.
    Your appearance is weighty, your raiment is of flame,
    your lips are fire as they utter.
    Who is able to speak with you?

11. "Your exalted manner of speech belongs elsewhere:
    why do you speak like us and with us?
    Your appearance is exalted and not of this earth;
    if there is some race of fiery beings
    then it is to it that you belong, O fearsome hero.

12. "O offspring of flame, explain to me
    the matter concerning which you speak,
    for you have announced a birth—yet I have known no man.
    Your message is fearsome, like yourself:
    your voice and your words are just like your appearance.

13. "How can there be a conception without a man?
    How can a virgin give birth?
    Who has ever beheld a crop without any seed?
    Explain to me what it is you are saying,
    how all this can possibly take place."

14. The Watcher replied, "It is the Holy Spirit   Lk 1.35
    who will come to you and make holy your womb;
    then the Power of the Most High shall descend and reside in
        you.
    From your womb shall Riches shine out
    —to pay all the debts of the world."   cf. Col 2.14

2. Nativity: Ephrem, Hymns on the Nativity, 17

Introduction

The poem opens with Mary describing her unique experience as
mother of such a wondrous Child. Unlike Eve, who "put on leaves of
shame," she puts on "a robe of glory," by virtue of bearing Christ. It is
not clear whether or not Mary continues to be the intended speaker
throughout the poem, though this seems likely (and is definitely so
in stanzas 8–11), in which case it is she herself who invites all sorts
of different categories of people to benefit from what her Son can
offer them.

    In stanza 2 "the high priest, the aged servant" refers to Simeon
who received the infant Christ in the Temple (Luke 2.25): he has
here been identified as Simeon the High Priest in Ben Sira (see the
Introduction to Ch. IV, no. 4). In the final stanzas Ephrem seeks to
refute the doctrine of those who held that the Creator of this world
was an inferior divine being, who was completely different from the
supreme God, the Father of Christ the Son.

Translation

1. "The tiny Child I carry himself carries me,"
   said Mary; "hee lowered his wings,
   took me and placed me between his pinions;
   he soared into the heavens, and promised me,
   'Both height and depth shall be your Son's.'

Refrain: Praise to you, Son of the Creator, who love all humanity.

2. "I saw Gabriel, and he called him 'Lord';   Lk 1.28
   and the high priest, the aged servant   Lk 2.25, 29
   —he carried him in honour; I saw the Magi
   —they bowed down to him; while Herod I saw   Mt 2.11,
   troubled, because the King had come.   Mt 2.3

3. "Satan, who slew the newborn of the Hebrews,   Ex 1.16
   wanting to destroy Moses, now kills the children, Mt 2.16
   hoping that Life will die. To Egypt will I flee,   Mt 2.13
   as Satan has come to Judaea to go toiling around
   trying to hunt his own Hunter.

4. "In her virginity Eve put on
   leaves of shame, but your mother has put on,   Gen 3.7
   in her virginity, a garment of glory
   that encompasses all humanity, while to him who covers all
   she gives a body as tiny raiment.

5. "Blessed is she, in whose heart and mind
   you are: she is a royal palace   cf. Prov 9.1
   —because of you, O royal Son. She is the Holy of Holies
   for you, the High Priest. She knows no worries
   or cares of home—or husband.

6. "Eve proved the cranny—and the sepulchre—
   for the accursed serpent: there entered her and dwelt there
   its evil counsel; she became its bread,   Gen 3.4–5
   since she had become dust. But you are our Bread,
   you are our bridal chamber, our robe of glory.

7. "Is any woman living in chastity afraid?
   —He shall preserve her. Has any some sin?
   —He shall forgive it. Has any some evil spirit?
   —He shall drive it out. For those with diseases
   here is One who will bandage up their fractured state.

8. "Has any woman a child? Let him come and be
   brother to my Beloved. Has any a daughter or niece?
   Let her come along and become
   the betrothed of my most honoured one. Has anyone a slave?
   Let him release him to come to serve his Lord.

9. "My Son, the free-born who bears your yoke
   has a single reward, while the servant who carries
   the double yoke of two masters,
   in heaven and on earth—he shall have two blessings,
   a double reward for his double burden.

10. "My Son, the free-born girl is your handmaid
    if she serves you, whereas a girl who is in slavery
    is free-born in you: in you she shall find comfort,
    for she has been liberated with that hidden freedom
    that is stored up in her bosom if she loves you.

11. "Chaste women, yearn for my Beloved,
    so that he may dwell in you. And you, too, who are unclean
    he wishes to make holy. The churches too
    he wants to adorn. Son of the Creator is he
    who has come to restore all creation.

12. "He has renewed the heaven, because foolish men
    had worshipped all sorts of stars; he has renewed the earth
    which had grown old in Adam. With his spittle   Jn 9.6
    there took place a novel fashioning:
    he who is capable of all things puts aright both bodies and
          minds.

13. "Come, all you who are blind, receive light
    without payment; come, you lame,
    receive back the use of your legs; you who are deaf and dumb,
    receive back the use of your voices;
    those whose hands are crippled shall also regain their use.

14. "He is the Creator's Son, whose treasure stores are filled
    with every benefit. he who needs eyes,
    let him approach him:
    he will fashion mud and transform it   Jn 9.6
    fashioning flesh and giving light to the eyes.

15. "With a little mud he showed how, through him,
    our dust was fashioned. The soul of the dead Lazarus, too,
    bore witness to him how, by him, a person's breath

                                  Jn 11.43–4
    is breathed into him. By these latter witnesses   Gen 2.7
    he is to be believed to be Son of God, the First Principle.

16. "Gather together and come, you lepers, receive cleansing
    without any trouble; for there is no need
    as in Elisha's case, of dipping seven times   2 Kg 5.14
    in the river Jordan: Christ does not tire people out any more
    with the sprinklings, as the priests did of old.   Lev 14.7

17. "Elisha's 'seven times' symbolizes the purification   2 Kg 5.10
    of the woman with seven spirits, while the hyssop and blood
                                  Lk 8.2; Lev 14.6

are powerful types too. There is no place here
for thinking that Christ is 'alien': Christ, the Son of the Lord
      of all,
is not alienated from the Lord of All.

18. "If it was the 'Just God' who made a body leprous,
      while you cleanse it, then the Fashioner of the body
      hated the body, while you loved it;
      but as it is, you fashioned it, and the bandages
      that you put on it cry out that you are the Creator's Son."

3. Epiphany: Hymns on Epiphany 6, attributed to Ephrem

Introduction

In the Eastern Christian Churches Epiphany is the Feast of the
Baptism of Christ, and not the visit of the Magi, as in Western
Christian tradition. Another title for it is Theophany, referring to the
manifestation of the Trinity at this event, where the dove denotes the
presence of the Spirit and the voice from heaven that of the Father.
Christ's Baptism is understood as providing one of the two main
fountain-heads of Christian Baptism, the other being Paul's view
in Romans 6, according to which Christ's death and resurrection
provide the other paradigm for Baptism. Syriac tradition would
more frequently link this second understanding with John 19.34, the
pierced side of Christ as he hung on the cross, and the issuing forth
of water and blood, seen as symbols of Baptism and Eucharist. But
this is not a case of either/or, for the two understandings comple-
ment, rather than contradict, one another: Christian Baptism is both
a rebirth (thus John 3.3) and a death and resurrection.

Since one strand of early Syriac tradition tended to give greater
emphasis to the idea that Christ's own Baptism was the source of
Christian Baptism, Baptisms were often performed at Epiphany

(rather than on the eve of the Resurrection, as tended to be the case elsewhere). Accordingly, in the following hymn for Epiphany we find references to the newly baptized as well as to Christ's own Baptism. It is interesting that some of the phraseology used of the newly baptized is still to be found in the Maronite baptismal rite.

Although this hymn is attributed to Ephrem, there are good reasons for doubting the correctness of this; on the other hand, it bears all the hallmarks of being a product of the late fourth century (the Holy Spirit is still treated grammatically as feminine, a feature I have reflected in the translation).[1]

Translation

1. The Spirit descended from the heights
   and sanctified the water as She hovered.
   When John baptized Jesus
   She left all others and settled on one,   Mt 3.16 and par.
   but now She has come down and settled
   upon all who are reborn in the water of Baptism.

2. Of all those that John baptized
   the Spirit dwelt on one alone,
   but now She has flown down
   to dwell upon many.
   Rushing to meet the Foremost who went up first from the
        Jordan,
   She embraced him and dwelt upon him.

[1]For the use of feminine imagery in connection with the Holy Spirit in early Syriac literature, see "'Come, compassionate Mother . . . come, Holy Spirit'; a forgotten aspect of early Eastern Christian imagery," in my *Fire from Heaven: Studies in Syriac Theology and Liturgy* (Aldershot, 2006), chapter VI.

3.   It is a wonder that the Purifier of all
     should have gone down to the water to be baptized.
     The seas declared that river blessed,
     in which you, Lord, were baptized.
     The waters, too, that are above in the heavens
     were envious that they had not been held worthy to wash you.

4.   It is a wonder, Lord, now as well
     that, though the springs are full of water,
     only the baptismal font
     can wash clean:
     the seas may be mighty with all their water,
     but they have not the power to wash.

5.   If your power, Lord, resides
     in something insignificant,
     then it grows, as part of the kingdom;
     if you reside in the wilderness, it receives peace.
     Through your power water has conquered sin,
     for Life has drowned it.

6.   The sheep leapt with joy to see
     the hand in readiness to baptize.
     O lambs, receive your marking,
     enter in and mingle with the flock:
     today the angels rejoice in you
     more than in all the rest of the sheep.

7.   Angels and Watchers rejoice
     at the birth effected by the Spirit and water:
     beings of fire and spirit rejoice,
     since those in the body have now become spiritual.
     The Seraphs who cry "Holy" rejoice   Is 6.2–3
     because the number of those who sing "Holy" is increased.

8. Since the angels rejoice
   at the single sinner who repents,   Lk 15.10
   how much more do they rejoice
   when at each feast and gathering
   Baptism gives birth
   to heavenly beings out of earthly.

9. The baptized who have come up from the water are
        sanctified,
   those who went down to it have been cleansed;
   those who have come up have been robed in praise,
   those who went down have stripped off sin.
   Adam stripped off glory all of a sudden;
   you have put on glory all of a sudden!

10. A house made of mud bricks, when it gets old,
    can be renovated by using water;
    so Adam's body, made of muddy earth,
    grew old and was renovated by water.
    The priests are like builders, you see,
    making new your bodies once more.

11. It is a great wonder that the wool
    which can receive every kind of dye
    —like the mind that receives all kinds of thoughts—
    takes on the very name of the dye
    —just as you were baptized as "hearers"
    and have now been named "partakers."

12. Elisha, using the hidden Name,   cf. 2 Kg 5.10
    sanctified ordinary water,
    and the leper Naaman who visibly dipped in them
    was cleansed by the Hidden Power: 2 Kg 5.14
    leprosy was destroyed in the water,
    just as sin is destroyed in Baptism.

13. Today your debts are wiped out,
    and your names are written down;
    the priest wipes them out in the water,
    and Christ writes your names in heaven.
    By the two actions
    your joy is redoubled.

14. Today mercy shines forth,
    stretching from extremity to extremity.
    The Sun of Righteousness was baptized: Mercy shone forth,

    Mal 4.2

    and Justice withdrew her anger;
    Grace stretched forth her love,
    freely giving mercy and salvation.

15. The older sheep within the fold
    have run to embrace
    the new lambs that have been added.
    You are white now; put on white garments,
    white both within and without—
    your bodies, like your clothes.

16. "Blessed are you," cries every tongue,
    for in every respect you are blessed:
    sin has been chased away from you,
    the Holy Spirit has resided upon you.
    Gloom fills the Evil One's face,
    joy the face of the person who is good.

17. You have received the gift freely   Mt 10.8
    —cease not in your watch over it,
    for if the pearl be lost,
    it cannot be sought out again:
    it resembles virginity,
    once lost, it cannot be recovered.

18. May the power of your white garments
    keep you pure from all stain.
    Tears can wash that person
    whose free will has defiled him.
    May the supplications of the community gain pardon
    for me who am the community's servant.

19. For the poet who has toiled with words
    may there be pardon through mercy;
    for the preacher who has toiled with speaking,
    may there be forgiveness through grace;
    for the priest who has toiled in the baptismal rite,
    may there be a crown through justice.

20. From the mouths of all, equally,
    both those on earth and those above,
    Watchers, Cherubim, and Seraphim,
    baptized, the anointed, and catechumens,
    let us all cry aloud,
    "Praise to the Lord of the Feasts!"

4. Epiphany: anonymous hymn

Introduction

Epiphany and Christ's Baptism were seen by many Syriac poets as the time of the betrothal of the Church to Christ, with John the Baptist acting as it were as the marriage broker. Although bridal imagery is very common in Ephrem and other early Syriac writers, this is derived entirely from the New Testament, and not from the Song of Songs, as one might initially have imagined. Imagery from the Song of Songs only starts to feature in the liturgical poetry in the early sixth century, and this may have then been due to the translation into Syriac, of about that time, of Gregory of Nyssa's Commentary, where the Song of Songs is interpreted throughout as referring to Christ the Bridegroom and the Church his Bride. In the present poem, which is full of allusions to the Song, the Church herself is the speaker. In the fourth stanza the unknown poet will have in mind a famous group of poems on the symbolism of the pearl by Ephrem (Hymns on Faith, 81–85).

Translation

1. God has summoned me to his marriage feast,
    says the Church to the invited guests,
    to enter with him into the Bridal Chamber.
    O Peoples, rejoice with me for I have been saved.

2. I have come up from the street full of idols   cf. Song 3.2
    and been baptized in the living water;   Song 4.15; Jn 4.10
    in Fire and Spirit have I been made to shine,
    and I am joined to the glorious Bridegroom.

3. I was in captivity and distraught
    among the mountains and the hills,   cf. Song 2.8, 4.6
    but he treated my wound with oil and with wine,   Lk 10.34
    and with the comfort he gave me I forgot all that had caused
        me to stumble.

4. I am like the pearl
    that was born under the water;
    the Holy Spirit descended and drew me up   cf. Ps 18.16
    to place me on the King's diadem.

5. The Bridegroom alighted from his Father's house
    to prepare the wedding feast for the Bride.

In the womb of the font
did he crown her and make her resplendent and pure.

6. Baptism, the daughter of light,
is the entry into God's presence;
a person who does not enter by it
cannot behold the Most High.

7. A rock in the wilderness provided   Ex 17.6; Num 20.8
water for the recalcitrant People,
designating for us the font
which has given life to mortals.

8. The thirst of the people in Ashimon   Deut 32.10
lasted until this rock, and then it was brought to an end;
likewise the death of our human race
reached as far as the cross, and then was finished off.

9. Mary became the head of the way
by which he went down to become dead himself,
while for us the font is the head
of the way which raises me up to heaven.

10. He fashioned Adam out of dust   Gen 3.19
and he became corrupted by sin.
But in the water of Baptism
he returned to his former state.

11. Because the serpent had stolen the clothes
of Adam, that fair image,   Gen 1.26–7
the royal Son brought them back
to reclothe Adam in his adornment.

12. The serpent led Eve astray   Gen 3.1–5
and stole away from her her crown,

but the Virgin's Son trampled down the serpent

Gen 3.15; Ps 74.14

and from the baptismal water gave back to Eve her crown.

13. His fragrant unguent has made my head shine,

Song 1.3; Ps 23.5

with his living Cup he has inebriated my heart.   Ps 23.5

His mercies are better than wine.   Song 1.2

Love him, all you who are upright, for he has taken delight in
    me.   Song 1.4

14. I was blackened in my sins   Song 1.5–6

as a result of sacrificial burnt offerings.

The daughter of Jerusalem has become jealous of me, Song 1.5

for I am glorious now that I have been made to shine.

15. Jesus is mine, and I am his.   Song 2.16

he has desired me: he has clothed himself in me, and I am
    clothed in him.

With the kisses of his mouth has he kissed me   Song 1.2

and brought me to his Bridal Chamber on high.   cf. Song 1.4

16. I went out after him and sought him,   Song 3.1, 5.7

but the guards of the night frightened me—   Song 3.3, 5.7

the demons who keep watch in the dark:

they despoiled me because I loved him.   Song 5.7

17. His appearance is fairer than that of anyone else,   cf. Is 53.3

his lips distil mercy,   Song 5.13

he resembles the grain-pile of life   Song 7.3

from which creation takes its fill.

18. He made me his Bride from the Jordan's water;

he gave me freedom from the water,

he showed me his Father's riches,
and look, his kingdom awaits me.

19. In the womb of the Virgin he betrothed me
    and he received me in pure union of marriage;
    he mingled me with his exalted nature
    and made me an heir of Life.

20. From the womb Jesus is mine,
    and I am his from the water.
    A pure Virgin has given him to me,
    and Baptism has given me to him.

21. He has cast in me the fire of his love:
    from the water it caught alight in me.
    With love of salvation I burn,
    to behold the Bridegroom I thirst.

22. With holy oil am I marked,
    with living water am I baptized,
    with the Spirit's circumcision am I circumcised,
    to the kingdom am I invited.

23. Like the coin out of the lake   Mt 17.27
    have I come up from the font;
    with Fire and Spirit have I been forged.
    I have entered the flock of the Son.

24. With garments of glory am I clothed,
    with raiment of light am I wrapped.
    From the water I have become a virgin,
    and behold, angels are rejoicing at me.   Lk 15.10

25. On my head has the Bridegroom placed his hand,

Song 2.6, 8.3

   and look, his right arm embraces me.
   Through the touch of his hand have I been reborn
   from the baptismal womb.

26. May I worship you, Lord, for you have saved me.
   Let my children give thanks, because you have brought me to
      Life.
   Let my mouth praise you, for in you does my heart rejoice:
   blessed are you, the source of peace to her who was desolate!

5. Lent: Ephrem, Hymns on the Fast, 6

Introduction

Lent, or the Great Fast, is a period for which numerous biblical readings are appointed. Ephrem here compares them to merchants offering their wares to humanity: different things are beneficial to different people. Everyone has been given access to this treasury belonging to God, but the inner eye of discernment is needed for making the right choice of what to take from it. Satan, however, has successfully blinded humanity's spiritual eye; as a result humanity is in need of the same sort of healing that Jesus effected with Bartimaeus in the Gospel of Mark (Ephrem assumes that Jesus acted in the same way as that described in John 9.6). The Voice in the first stanza will be John the Baptist, who publicly proclaims Christ, thus providing the hermeneutical key to understanding the symbols and types in the Old Testament.

Translation

1. In the midst of the Fast the Scriptures have gathered together
    and become merchants,
    having in their possession a veritable treasure store of
    divinity.
    With that holy Voice as the key
    they are opened up before those who will listen.
    Blessed is that King who has opened up his treasury to his
    people!

2. Here are to be found garments for those invited to the
    wedding feast;   Mt 22.11
    here, too, are sackcloth and tears for all kinds of penitents;
    here in their midst is one who sustains the athletes as well;
    with every kind of riches are they filled.
    Blessed is he who has prepared for everyone every kind of
    succour!

3. Open up then, my brethren, and take from it with
    discernment,
    for this treasure store is the common property of everyone,
    and each person, as if he were treasurer, possesses his own
    key.
    Who can fail to get rich?
    Blessed is he who has removed the cause of our low estate!

4. Great is that gift which is set down before our blind eyes:
    for even though we all have a pair of eyes each,
    few are those who have perceived that gift,
    who are aware of what it is and from whom it comes.
    Have mercy, Lord, on the blind, for all they can see is gold!

5. O Jesus, who opened the eyes of Bartimaeus,   Mk 10.46
    you opened his eyes that had become blind against his will;

open, Lord, the eyes that of our own free will
we have rendered blind; thus shall your grace abound.
The mud that you made then, Lord, tells us that you are the
    Son of our Maker.   Jn 9.6

6. Who is there like you, who gave such honour to our faces?
   For it was upon the ground that you spat, and not upon his
     face,
   thus holding our image in honour.   Gen 1.27
   But with us, please spit on our faces, Lord, and open the eyes
     which our own free will has closed.
   Blessed is he who gave the mind's eye—which we have
     managed to blind.

7. Who can fail to wonder at Adam, and how his eyes were
     opened: Gen 3.7
   in Adam's case their opening proved harmful,
   but we, Lord, if our eyes were opened, would be greatly
     benefited,
   seeing that it was the Evil One who has closed them.
   Blessed is he who gave succour and both closed and opened
     up eyes!

8. Who can fail to curse that thorn that betrayed us,

                                              2 Cor 12.7
   who by cunning opened up Adam's eyes so that he beheld his
     own shame;   Gen 3.7
   he has beguiled us too and smeared over our eyes
   so that we might not see the enormity of our naked state.
   Curse him, Lord, at the hand of all, so that you may be
     blessed by all.

6. Resurrection: Jacob of Serugh, hymn

Introduction

According to Mark 16.1 and Luke 24.1 women brought spices to the tomb of Christ, and among them, according to Mark, were two Marys: Mary Magdalene and Mary the mother of James. In John 20.1, however, it is just Mary Magdalene who comes, and no mention is made of the fragrant spices. Liturgical tradition tended to fuse the different Gospel accounts, and at the same time make use of an early tradition (already encountered in Chapter IV, no. 12) that it was Mary, the mother of Jesus, who mistook the risen Christ for the Gardener (John 20.15), and not Mary Magdalene. In the present hymn it would seem very likely that Jacob of Serugh is also making use of this tradition, and that it is Mary the mother of Jesus who is the speaker.

Translation

1. The disciples fled from the beloved Master,
   but the guards remained by the luminous tomb.

   Mt 27.64–66

   The women disciples brought spices,
   fragrant herbs, to the tomb of the Fair One: Mk 16.1, Lk 24.1
   the chaste women came with their fragrances together with
       the tears of their eyes.

2. The chaste women came, carrying fragrant herbs
   as a wedding gift for the Bridal Chamber of the One who was
       slain.
   The Bridegroom came forth in glory
   from the tomb, and the guards were put to shame
   —but Mary did not realize that her Beloved had arisen.

3. She came to the tomb with the band of her companions;
    they trembled in dismay that he had been taken from the
        tomb.   Mk 16.5, 8
    "Where is the Light of all creation?
    Where is humanity's Sun?   cf. Mal 4.2
    Who has taken the Luminary? Where is he hidden?

4. "Tell me, O tomb, where is my Lord who came to you?
    Who has dared to steal away the very Flame?
    Has heaven snatched away the Son of its Lord?
    Or has the earth taken him, or the sea?
    O all creation, handmaids, search with me for the Only-
        Begotten."

5. The Free-born One has slept among the dead of his own free
        will,   Ps 88.5
    and his Father did not wish to leave his Beloved
    to see corruption in the tomb: Acts 2.27, 31; 13.37
    he has arisen, and his guards are put to shame,
    while the blessed woman asks who has taken her Beloved!

6. The angels came down from the heights above
    and stood beside the tomb in white raiment.
                              Mk 16.5, Lk 24.4; Jn 20.11
    The tomb became a beauteous Bridal Chamber
    for the supernal beings who came down and saw it.
    The guards were reproached by the angels' descent.

7. The angels entered that tomb of wonder
    and looked in amazement at the Hero's couch:
    he had been laid here of his own will,
    yet the heavens are filled with his praises.
    Here the Watchful One slept, while his ministers do not sleep!

8. The angels stood at his head and feet,   Jn 20.12
    but these supernal beings did not dare to tread
    on that place where the Hero had reclined,
    for they trembled at it, holding it in honour,
    so as not to desecrate the bed of him who measured out their
        ranks.

9. The angels saw as the chaste women wept;
    they replied to their questions with zeal,
    "O women, why do you weep, whom are you looking for
        here?   Jn 20.13; Lk 24.5
    This is the place of the departed,
    whereas your Master is the Resurrection itself.

10. "Why is the Living One being sought for among the dead?
                                                 Lk 24.5
    Why should the Luminary be in a place of darkness?
    The Dead One who resurrects the dead, is not here;
    he has carried out his word, he has returned to his Father's
        house.
    O Mary, do not weep over the Living One who resurrects all!"

11. The Lord of Paradise is risen from the tomb,
    and Mary saw him and likened him to the gardener.   Jn 20.15
    He *is* the Gardener who planted Paradise
    and encircled it with the sword and the cherub.   Gen 3.24
    You did well, O Mary, to call him "Gardener"!

12. Mary says, "Come to your garden, O gardener,
    come and look for the Fruit I have lost in your garden.
    If you have taken him from the tomb,   Jn 20.15
    show me where he is laid in your garden.
    The Jews will not consent to me, so give him to me that I may
        have joy in him.

13. "O gardener, how fair is your garden,
    in it is a tomb where, like the sovereign of the trees,
    is the Fruit of true salvation
    which the day before yesterday was suspended on the wood;
    now It is here: come, let us look for It so that we may enjoy Its
        taste.

14. "O gardener, if you have taken delight in It and carried It off,
    show me where the fair Fruit is placed;
    give It to me that I may take It from hence,
    from this garden of yours, so full of treasures.
    Do not hold me back, O gardener; give It to me, for It is my
        due."

15. Our Lord was pleased to be likened to a gardener,
    for it is he who opened the gate of Paradise for people to
        enter in;
    it was he who broke the cherub's sword,   Gen 3.24
    and thus the banished Adam entered into his inheritance.
    Rightly did he resemble a gardener at his resurrection!

16. He called out to her, "Mary," and at his voice she was
        illumined: Jn 20.16
    her understanding lit up, and she yearned for him, the
        Daylight.
    The darkness of sufferings was dispersed
    at the sight of the luminous Sun;   cf. Mal 4.2
    her countenance, clouded over at his death, now at his
        resurrection lit up.

7. Resurrection: anonymous hymn

Introduction

From the overall perspective of salvation history, the nativity, the resurrection and the ascension of Christ represent three focal points, and these are here represented by the months in which they fall. June also represents the month of the wheat harvest, and so provider of the flour from which to make "the Bread of New Life."

Translation

1. April is crowned with flowers,
   and on his shoulders is the resurrection of the Son.
   Here is December with his lap full of lullabies
   for the birth of the Child who is older than all.
   June escorts him at the mystery of his ascension;
   for the months minister to the Lord of all the months:
   one gave him birth, another resurrection,
   yet another exalted him, raising him up again to heaven.

2. Three wondrous events occur in these three months,
   three hidden mysteries belong to these three:
   December liberates from slavery,
   April dissolves the cold, and June the darkness,
   strangling it as it is removed:
   in June the sun is raised up to the zenith,
   and shines right down into the wells;
   in it our Sun was exalted, and his light has shone in the dark
        cleft.   Mal 4.2

3. At your nativity creation rejoiced,
   at your resurrection the Church was brought salvation,

at your ascension the race of Adam
was lifted up from death's abyss.
Blessed is your nativity, Lord, glorious is your resurrection;
blessed is your ascension, resplendent your exaltation.
Your Father, together with your Spirit, is to be worshipped:
he gave us you so that through you we might revive from
  death.

4. December offers you, O Church, in his bosom
the birth of the heavenly Child;
rejoice on meeting him, and sing out to him,
keep vigil and give thanks on the day he shone forth.
April offers you his death and resurrection,
hasten then yourself, acting in suffering and joy.
In June when he was raised up,
raise up to him the Bread of New Life!

5. See how the feasts and months encircle you,
O glorious queen of queens.
In your bosom you carry the blessings of Abraham,
the priesthood of Levi and his birthright.
The prophets bore symbols, the apostles glorious acts:
they have poured them out into your lap, raining them down
  on your children
—and on me too, ugly though I am,
sprinkle some of your blessed dew!

6. Adorn me too, Lord, in your good will,
for my own self-will has made me utterly ugly;
for the face's beauty is something that belongs to nature,
but inner beauty of heart is a matter of the will.
O Good One who, in your grace, have adorned nature,
and adorned humanity, too, with the garment of free will,
have pity on me, Lord, in my weakness,

and may I enter that Bridal Chamber of yours, clothed in
your raiment.

8. Salvation history: Jacob of Serugh, Hymn on the Soul

Introduction

The Soul, who is at first addressed, and then speaks, is a representative of every human soul, and the poem thus associates each individual with the pattern of salvation. The poem (which has an alphabetic acrostic) falls into three parts:

Stanzas 1–7: the Soul is reproved;
stanzas 8–15: the Soul replies;
stanzas 16–22: the Soul is comforted.

The identity of the speaker in the first and third sections is left unspecified. Throughout the poem, the soul's experience is related in terms of the Fall of Adam/humanity, and the characteristically Syriac theme of the Robe of Glory—lost at the Fall, and then made available again thanks to the incarnation—is alluded to on several occasions.

Translation

1. O Soul, depiction of the kingdom,
   who has stripped you of your beauty and mocked you?
   For look how ugly you are with your many evil deeds.

2. In Paradise full of blessings you were resplendent
   as you reclined in glorious delights.
   Who is it who has cast you down into the land of the curses?

   Gen 3.17

3.   The King chose you and brought you into his chamber;

Song 1.3

he revealed his wealth, and showed you his treasure,
so why is it you have shown hate for him who is rich?

2 Cor 8.9

4.   It is a matter of astonishment that instead of living close
to the glorious light of Paradise,
of your own will you have loved darkness instead.

5.   The halleluiahs and cries of "holy" of those above   Is 6.3
and the glorious ministry of spiritual beings
you have abandoned—and gone after wild animals!

6.   Alas, O Soul, neighbour of the Luminous One,
image of the Great One, how far has your fallen state reached!

Gen 1.26–7

For now thorns are mingled for you in your bread.

Gen 3.18–19

7.   You were clothed in rays of light,
you were sealed with the King's own necklace;
who is it that has given you leaves to cover your nakedness?

Gen 3.7

THE SOUL SPEAKS

8.   The Accursed One laid ambush and mocked me;
he stole my clothes, and so I stood naked.   Gen 3.7
Now, with the leaves he has clothed me in, I am scorned.

9.   I went astray because I listened to the Evil One: Gen 3.13
in his guile he led me into captivity,
and now my feet are entangled in his stumbling blocks.

10. I should have kept the commandment, Gen 2.16
    but I did not keep it; for that reason I am thrown down
    in the place of thorns, and my captor mocks me. Gen 3.18

11. He laid ambush and craftily set a snare,
    he made me suppose that he would give me greatness,
    but when I came close, he threw me into the pit.

12. He enticed me on, saying he would raise me to heaven,
    whereas he dug for me a grave—into which I fell,
    and now I lie in Sheol, the home of the dead.

13. I went wrong because of the beauty of the Tree; Gen 3.6
    its beauty was borrowed, and I did not realize,
    but when I tried it, how I shook and felt ashamed!

14. He made me a guardian for Paradise, Gen 2.15
    but I failed to guard it—and so I am despised,
    for I stole the very fruit which has now killed me.

15. The Slayer of humanity has gone after me,
    jealous at my beauties which were many.
    Through his cunning he has destroyed me—what can I now
        do?

THE SOUL IS COMFORTED

16. With you is the hope of all creation:
    O Soul, do not cut off all hope,
    for the Tree of Life is beside you.

17. There has flown down and come from Eden of the luminous
        ones
    that Fruit, the Lover of humanity.
    Rise up and eat of it: revive, you who were dead!

18. He has caught and slain the serpent that mocked you,
    He has crushed its head, seeing that it had deceived you.

    Ps 74.14

    Return, O Soul, to Eden, which is gazing out for you.

19. The serpent is slain, the Accursed One is crushed,
    broken is the sword of the guardian cherub.   Gen 3.24
    O Daughter of Light, come and enter into Paradise!

20. Your greatness and your beauty that were lost
    —all this you have now found on the height of Golgotha.
    Arise, clothe yourself and return to your inheritance.

21. Strip off your rags and the leaves that cover your nakedness;
    take and put on the glorious robe,
    enter into Eden which is opened up and awaits you.

22. That garment which the serpent stole from you
    the King's Son has brought and given to you.
    Praise be to him who has returned you to your Father's house.

9. Baptism: anonymous baptismal hymn.

Introduction

At Baptism the font is seen as representing the river Jordan, in which Christ, at his own Baptism, had deposited the "garment of glory" which Adam and Eve had lost as a result of their disobedience in eating of the forbidden fruit (Gen 2.17), but which was now available for human beings to put on again in potential at Christian Baptism. Baptism is thus a return to Paradise, but a Paradise now enhanced because the fruit of the Tree is no longer forbidden, but freely given, it being nothing else than Christ's own eucharistic Body. Furthermore, the newly baptized, wearing white, receive wedding crowns, since Baptism is an anticipation of the eschatological Wedding Feast, with the entry into the heavenly Bridal Chamber of joys for those whose souls who have been kept pure, in company with the Wise Virgins (Mt 25.10). The twenty-two stanzas form an alphabetical acrostic.

Translation

1. Make your garments glisten,
   my brothers and sisters, like snow;
   make your radiance beautiful,
   like that of the angels.

2. In the likeness of the angels
   have you gone up, my beloved,
   from Jordan's river,
   clothed in the armour of the Holy Spirit.   cf. Eph 6.11

3. You have received, my sisters and brothers,
   the Bridal Chamber that never fades;

and today you have put on
Adam and Eve's lost glory.

4. That judgement which resulted from the forbidden fruit

                                                    Gen 2.17, 3.11

    showed Adam to be guilty,
    whereas for you this day
    victory has ascended.

5. How resplendent are your garments,
    how lovely are your crowns
    that the Firstborn has plaited for you
    this day at the hands of the priest!

6. It was woes that Adam
    in Paradise received,   Gen 3.17
    but you have received
    glory this day.

7. Armour of victory
    did you put on, my beloved,
    at that moment when the priest
    invoked the Holy Spirit.

8. Angels rejoice
    and those below exult
    at your wedding feast, my brothers and sisters,
    wherein there is no impurity.

9. Heaven's blessed state
    have you received, my sisters and brothers:
    be wary of the Evil One   1 Pet 5.8
    lest he strip you bare!

10. The day upon which
    the Heavenly King has shone forth
    opens up its door for you
    and brings you into Eden.

11. Crowns that never fade
    have been placed upon your heads;
    let your tongues at every moment
    sing out in praise!

12. Because of the fruit
    God sent Adam forth in sorrow,   Gen 3.23
    whereas you God causes to rejoice
    in the Bridal Chamber of joy.

13. Who would not rejoice
    at your Bridal Chamber, my brothers and sisters?
    For there the Father rejoices
    with his Child and the Spirit.

14. The Father shall be for you
    a mighty wall of protection,
    the Son a Savior,
    and the Spirit a guardian.

15. The martyrs, with their blood,
    made their crowns resplendent,
    but in your case our Savior
    has made you resplendent with his own blood.

16. The Watchers and Angels
    rejoice over the penitent,   Lk 15.10
    Let them rejoice in you, my sisters and brothers,
    for you have become like them!

17. The fruit which Adam
    never tasted in Paradise
    has been placed this day
    in your very mouths, a cause of joy!

18. Our Savior depicted
    his Body in the Tree
    from which Adam never tasted   Gen 3.22
    as a result of his sin.

19. The Evil One made battle
    and defeated both Adam and Eve,
    but today at your Baptism,
    my brothers and sisters, he has been defeated.

20. Great is the victory
    which you have received this day
    —provided you are not neglectful,
    my sisters and brothers, or fail to be watchful.

21. Praise to him who has clothed
    Adam's children in glory
    at this rebirth from water:
    may we rejoice and receive blessing.

22. Thanksgiving to him who has clothed
    his churches in glory;
    praise be to him who has exalted
    Adam and Eve's family.

10. Eucharist: Ephrem, Hymns on Faith, 10

Introduction

In this eucharistic hymn Ephrem uses two Gospel examples to indicate the awe in which Christ's Body should be approached: John the Baptist even held Jesus' sandals in awe, while the woman with the flux wanted only to touch his garment in order to be healed. Since the standard early Syriac metaphor for the incarnation is "he put on the body," Christ's physical body can also be described as the garment of his divinity. Ephrem goes on to compare the "Hidden Power" that resided in his garment with the same "Hidden Power" that resides in the Bread and the Cup, consecrated by "Fire and the Spirit." Divine Fire, as several Old Testament passages indicated, is a source of awe, since it can have two different effects: it can either sanctify or destroy. A quotation from Proverbs (understood as being by Solomon) provides Ephrem with a means of introducing three new places where this divine Fire is present: Mary's womb, the river Jordan, and the baptismal font (sometimes actually referred to as the "Jordan" in Syriac tradition). At both the opening and at the end of the poem Ephrem compares himself to the Syro-Phoenician woman who was content with the crumbs that fall from the table: in Ephrem's case here, they prove even more than enough.

Translation

1. You have had it written, Lord, "Open your mouth and I will
   fill it." Ps 81.10
   Look, your servant's mouth is open, and his mind as well;
   fill it, Lord, with your Gift,
   that I may sing your praise in accordance with your will.

Refrain: Make me worthy to approach your Gift in awe!

2. Each, according to the level of his own measure, can tell of
        you;
    in my boldness I approach the lowest step.
    Your birth is sealed up within silence,
    what tongue then dares to meditate on it?

3. Your nature is single, but there are many ways of explaining
        it;
    our descriptions may be exalted, or in moderate terms, or
        lowly.
    Make me worthy of the lowest part, that I may gather up, as
        crumbs,
    the gleanings of all your wisdom.   Mt 15.27; Mk 7.28

4. Any elevated account of you is hidden with him who begot
        you;
    at your lesser riches the angels stand amazed,
    while a small trickle of words describing you, Lord,
    provides a flood of homilies for mortals below.

5. For if the great John cried out and said,
    "I am not worthy, Lord, of the straps of your sandals,"   Mk 1.7
    then I should take refuge, like the Sinful Woman,
                                                    Mt 9.21; Lk 8.47
    in the shadow of your garment and there begin.

6. And as she was affrighted, but took courage because she was
        healed,
    so do you heal my fear and my fright, and so I may take
        courage in you
    and be conveyed from your garment to your own Body,
    so that I may tell of it according to my ability.

7. Your garment, Lord, is a fountain of medicines:
   in your visible clothing there dwells your Hidden Power.
   Again, a little spittle from your mouth became   Jn 9.6
   a great miracle of light, for light was in the clay it made.

8. In your Bread there is hidden the Spirit who is not consumed,
   in your Wine there dwells the Fire that is not drunk:
   the Spirit is in your Bread, the Fire in your Wine—
   a manifest wonder, that our lips have received.

9. When the Lord came down to earth to mortal beings,
                                         2 Cor 5.17; Gal. 6.15
   he created them again, in a new creation, like the angels,
   mingling within them fire and spirit,
   so that in a hidden manner they might be of Fire and Spirit.

10. The Seraph could not touch the fire's coal with his fingers,
                                                         Is 6.6–7
    the coal only just touched Isaiah's mouth:
    the Seraph did not hold it, Isaiah did not consume it,
    but our Lord has allowed us to do both!

11. To the angels who are spiritual Abraham brought
                                                     Gen 18.8–9
    food for the body, and they ate. The new miracle
    is that our mighty Lord has given to bodily men
    Fire and Spirit to eat and to drink.

12. Fire descended in wrath and consumed the sinners;
                                                     Gen 19.24
    the Fire of Mercy has now descended and dwelt in the Bread:
    instead of that fire which consumed mankind
    you have consumed Fire in the Bread—and you have come to
        life!

13. Fire descended and consumed Elijah's sacrifices;   1 Kg 18.38
    the Fire of Mercies has become a living sacrifice for us;
    fire consumed Elijah's oblation,
    but we, Lord, have consumed your Fire in your Oblation.

14. Who has ever held in his cupped hands the wind?   Prov 30.4
    Come and see, Solomon, what the Lord of your father has
          done: cf. Ps 110.1
    against nature, he has mingled fire and spirit
    and poured them out in the hands of his disciples.

15. "Who has gathered up water in a veil?" he asked.   Prov 30.4
    Here is a Fountain in a veil—that is, Mary's bosom.
    And your maidservants receive, within a veil,
    the Drop of Salvation from Salvation's Cup.

16. There is a Hidden Power within the sanctuary's veil,
    a power that no mind has ever confined:
    it has brought down its love, descended and hovered
    over this veil on the altar of reconciliation.

17. See, Fire and Spirit are in the womb of her who bore you,
    see, Fire and Spirit are in the river in which you were
          baptized.
    Fire and Spirit are in our baptismal font,
    in the Bread and the Cup are Fire and Holy Spirit.

18. Your Bread slays the greedy one who had made us his bread;
    your Cup destroys death who had swallowed us up;
    we have eaten you, Lord, we have drunken you—
    not that we will consume you up, but through you we shall
          have Life.

19. The thong of your sandal is something fearful to the
      discerning,
    the hem of your cloak is awesome to those who understand,
    yet our foolish generation, through its prying into you,
    has gone quite mad, drunk with new wine.

20. There is wonder in your footsteps which walked upon the
      water: Mt 14.25
    you subjected a great sea beneath your feet,
    yet your head was subject to just a small river,
    in that it bent down and was baptized therein.

21. The river resembled John, who baptized in it:
    each reflects the other in its smallness;
    yet to the small river and to the weak servant
    was the Master of them both subjected!

22. Lord, my lap is now filled with the crumbs from your Table.
                                 Mk 7.28
    there is no more room in the folds of my garment,
    so stay your gift, as I worship before you:
    keep it in your treasure-house in readiness to give us on
      another occasion.

11. Marriage: anonymous marriage hymn

Introduction

Paul already considered that Christian marriage should be modelled
on the relationship of Christ to the Church (Eph 5.31–2), and in
subsequent Christian tradition the Church is frequently depicted as
the Bride of Christ. In the following marriage hymn the Church as
bride addresses Christ, her Bridegroom, using imagery taken from
the Song of Songs.

Translation

1. You are the Youth who has betrothed me,
   the mighty Planter of Eden: Gen 2.8
   blow upon me a sweet breeze   Song 4.16
   from your gardens that refresh me.

2. I am your betrothed, Lord,
   the bride who has been betrothed in your name;
   O Bridegroom of truth and reality,
   have pity on me for in you I have taken refuge.

3. On your cross you put a seal on my dowry
   and by your sufferings you have freed me;
   a Bridal Chamber on high have you set up for me
   and invited me that I should be yours.

4. Robbers fell upon me   cf. Song 5.7
   and wanted to destroy my beauty,
   but in your love you drove them away
   and I was delivered from servitude.

5. I exult in your love, O Lord,
   I rejoice in your beauty and delight,
   for I know that you are God's Son.
   O my Lord, take me into your arms!

6. It is in your love, my Lord, that I take refuge,
   and with desire for you do I burn.
   Place your left hand under my head   Song 2.6
   and with your right hand embrace me.

7. My Lord, do not be distant from me,
   do not deprive me of your company:

if you neglect your handmaid,
I shall fade away and die.

8. Your radiance is brighter than the sun,
   your fragrance sweeter than roses;
   your kisses are never enough,   Song 1.2
   for it is very life that your lips distil.   cf. Song 5.13

9. Look upon me, my Lord, for I am beautiful,   Song 1.5
   bring me into your chamber;   Song 1.4
   let me doze off and sleep in your bosom,
   a sleep that is sweet and delightful.

10. Blessed am I when they say to me,
    "Christ the Bridegroom who has betrothed you
    has risen in glory from the tomb"
    —and they came and announced this to me!

11. For days, months, and years
    did I dwell in the darkness of error,
    but when I heard your living voice,
    my eyes lit up, and my heart rejoiced.

12. Death: anonymous dialogue between the Soul and the Body

Introduction

Disputes between the Soul and the Body are to be found in both the medieval West and the Syriac Orient. No fewer than four poems survive in Syriac, indicating the popularity of the topic. A passage in Ephrem implies that disputes between Soul and Body were already known in his day:

> Body and Soul go to court
> to see which caused the other to sin.
> The wrong belongs to both,
> for free will belongs to both.
>
> (Nisibene Hymns, 69:5)

The relationship between Soul and Body, and how they influenced each other, had already been a matter of discussion in Greek philosophy; and in some strands of early Christianity, influenced especially by Plato, the body is assigned a very inferior role. Syriac writers, however, normally have a much more positive (and biblical) attitude towards the body. This is certainly the case in the following poem where the Soul, boasting of its "exalted nature" (stanza 21) is presented as constantly blaming the Body for being the source of all wrongdoing. The Body's response is to point out that, although Satan has used the Body as a vehicle for sins, these sins would never have taken place without the Soul's consent; furthermore, it will be a single sentence on them both that the Judge will eventually issue (stanza 40). The Soul, in its over-confidence, finally turns to the Judge and asks him to settle the case, and to grant it the crown which it is expecting (stanza 43). The Judge's reply, in stanzas 45–46, tacitly makes the Body the winner of the argument.

Translation

1. Soul and Body fell into dispute
   and became engaged in a great struggle.
   Let us now listen to what they are saying
   in that great contest in which they are engaged.

   Refrain: Praise to you, Lord, at whose advent
   sinners were saved from their wickedness
   and entered the protection of the Garden of Eden
   which is the holy Church.

2. News of this contest frightens me
   as they lay blame on one another;
   let us listen in truth to both sides
   like an unwavering judge.

3. SOUL: The Soul says, I never sinned
   or turned aside to evil deeds.
   Punish the Body, O Judge;
   do not smite me, for I have done no wrong.

4. BODY: The Body says, you shall be beaten together with me
   if Justice is judging us,
   for without you I would have done no wrong.
   Why should I have the stripes and you enjoy the Garden?

5. SOUL: It was in you, Body, that all the evil passions
   sprang up: they did not touch me.
   The lusts issued from you,
   that is why it is you who are to be chastised.

6. BODY: It was in you, Soul, that I was stirred up,
   I received my sensation in you;

had your emotions not come down to me
passions would never have harmed me.

7. SOUL: It is quite clear that my nature is exalted,
   above both passions and lust:
   the spirit is not subjected to passions—
   it is from you, Body, that all these spring forth.

8. BODY: It is quite clear that you will be beaten along with me,
   provided the Judge is not swayed,
   for though your nature is more exalted than mine,
   yet you consented with me to sin in evil deeds along with me.

9. SOUL: Mine is the crown, while it is you who are at fault,
   for I took no delight in evil deeds:
   I was grieved when you did wrong,
   but I was unable to prevent you from doing this wrong.

10. BODY: The stripes are due to me, as you say,
    but if I am beaten, you will be too,
    for had you not clothed yourself in me, there would have
       been
    no means by which I could suffer; why then do you try to
       escape?

11. SOUL: The upright Judge is aware
    that I hated wickedness with all my strength,
    and since it was not I who have done it, why should I
    be beaten along with you, Body, as you assert?

12. BODY: The Judge whom you have just invoked
    will see that I fasted and made supplication;
    how is it right that I should have toiled with this
    while you receive the reward for this toil of mine?

13. SOUL: You ought to know concerning this fast of yours
    that it was I who compelled you to come to it;
    I had to lead you as it were by force
    to that profitable labor against your own will.

14. BODY: You ought to be beaten along with me in all this;
    as you say that you have the strength,
    then why did you keep quiet when I did wrong by you,
    while failing to rebuke me?

15. SOUL: Our Judge is just, and I have no fear;
    I am quite confident that I will not be condemned:
    adultery and murder sprung forth from you,
    and so it is you who should stand for castigation.

16. BODY: He is just and upright and will see of me
    that once you left me I committed no adultery:
    in you was I stirred to lust,
    but once you had let go of me I was silent and quiet.

17. SOUL: I am related to the angels, so be quiet,
    whereas you are of dust; why then do you dispute?
    All ills spring from you,
    so why do you lay the blame on me?

18. BODY: You may be related to the angels, as you say,
    and I am dust, but you were in agreement with me,
    so along with dust you shall be punished
    since you, like it, have also done wrong.

19. SOUL: The crafty Evil One who has brought you low
    laid hidden snares for you, and into them you fell;
    but as for me, the snares did not affect me,
    and so I am not liable for castigation.

20. BODY: The Hateful One laid snares for me,
    but without you I would never have fallen in;
    you were illumined, but you never showed me
    where the trap lay so that I would not be caught.

21. SOUL: The Just One gave me a nature exalted
    above backslidings, and one that does not waver.
    He will hold me innocent, since he is most just;
    he will not associate me with your folly.

22. BODY: He gave you a mind and made you
    like a wise master for me:
    you did harm to the child who was entrusted to you,
    and so you stand liable to castigation.

23. SOUL: When you committed adultery, Body,
    your filth never touched me since my nature is exalted.
    How then is it just that the Requiter for adultery
    should punish me who did no wrong?

24. BODY: When I was asleep and you were on guard,
    who was the adulterer in that still sleep?
    You are the guard, why then did you not prevent
    that adulterous dream from defiling me?

25. SOUL: I did not consent when you did wrong,
    so I will be far away when you are beaten.
    You will be punished in your dust,
    while I will find delight in the sky.

26. BODY: You will not be far away when punishment comes
    if that Judge is not swayed,
    for had the body not been stirred by the soul to sin,
    it would never have sinned.

27. SOUL: Defects do not affect the soul,
    ulcers do not touch the spirit;
    sins and wrongs and all kinds of faults
    are yours, Body, so now keep quiet.

28. BODY: All the defects that are to be found in me
    would not have occurred, Soul, but for you,
    for when I felt lust, if you had wanted
    you could have restrained me from that lust.

29. SOUL: My Judge shall behold me and free me
    from blame as he condemns you.
    Because you delighted in dissipation,
    because you were eating away, am I to be accused?

30. BODY: My Judge shall behold me, and he will not separate
    you from your mate when he is punished,
    for had you not concurred and agreed with me,
    no wrong would ever have been done.

31. SOUL: The angels will testify that they do not backslide
    from that great state to which they belong;
    my nature is far above backslidings,
    for I am spirit, and I do not sin.

32. BODY: My Judge will testify how the demons backslid
    and fell from their place;
    they were of spirit, but because they fell away,
    behold Gehenna awaits them.

33. SOUL: Do not try to associate me with your evils,
    for I am far removed from all of them.
    All good deeds were done by me,
    so how is it right you should be held equal with me?

34. BODY: With those good deeds—if you have any—
    I am associated, so do not consider me separate:
    we are companions, and you cannot get away
    from your mate when he is punished.

35. SOUL: Let Paul come and teach you
    how spirit is not subjected to body:
    the body's lust may vanquish the spirit,   Gal. 5.17
    but it is the spirit's own lust which causes it harm.

36. BODY: Let Paul come along: you listen to him to see
    if my lust just harms me.
    No, for the wrong I have done you will be smitten,
    if I have erred, then harm comes to you.

37. SOUL: My will is most pure,
    excellent, good, wise, and exalted,
    and if the will is judged along with you, Body,
    then I will not receive a beating.

38. BODY: Your will is exalted, but I never constrained it
    in anything at all when I did wrong;
    for if you had never consented too,
    no wickedness would ever have been done.

39. SOUL: The Judge's voice is awesome indeed,
    and when he gives sentence he will begin all at once
    to separate out between you, Body, and me
    with truth upright, which cannot be swayed.

40. BODY: In his very presence shall it begin at once:
    a single command will he issue for us,
    and in his sentence he will not separate you off,
    for upright, just, and unswayed is he.

41. SOUL: My senses are exalted and I am raised high
    above those ills which come from you.
    This is quite fitting, that you should be chastised
    and I escape from any harm.

42. BODY: Your senses are exalted, but in me were you stirred
    in any good acts that may have been done:
    I acted as your tool and you spoke through me.
    The Judge is just and he will not keep you separate.

43. SOUL: Listen, O Judge, and settle the case all at once
    between me and the Body which utters such threats.
    Let truth shine out, O you who examine all,
    and grant me the crown which I expect.

44. BODY: Listen, Lord, and see: if the Soul receives a crown,
    do not deprive me;
    and if I am beaten, strike the Soul too,
    for without it I would never have sinned.

45. JUDGE: It is just that you both be punished
    if you have done wrong, so do not dispute;
    it is right that you both be crowned,
    and a single crown is reserved for you.

46. JUDGE: Both of you now have acted together,
    and a single judgement is reserved for you.
    Join one another and do not be separated,
    for there is no division between you.

47. Just is your judgement, O Lord of all;
    in mercy chastise both Body and Soul,
    have pity on them both when you manifest yourself
    in that kingdom which passes not away.

Sources

Further reading concerning the texts translated in this volume can usually be found in the sources listed below (the opportunity has been taken to make a few minor alterations in those cases where I have made use of my earlier translations). An excellent introduction to the early Syriac tradition is to be found in Robert Murray's *Symbols of Church and Kingdom* (Cambridge, 1975; new edition, Piscataway, NJ, 2004), and for the Syriac Bible information can be found in my *The Bible in the Syriac Tradition* (Piscataway, NJ, 2006).

III. Old Testament

1. Edition and translation in my "A Syriac dispute poem: the river Pishon and the river Jordan," in *Parole de l'Orient* 23 (1998), pp. 3–12.

2–3. Edition by E. Beck, *Des heiligen Ephraem des Syrers Hymnen de Paradiso und contra Julianum* (Corpus Scriptorum Christianorum Orientalium, Scriptores Syri 78; Louvain, 1957). There is a translation of the entire cycle in my *St Ephrem, Hymns on Paradise* (Crestwood, NY, 1990).

4. Edition, translation and commentary in my "Two Syriac dialogue poems on Abel and Cain," in *Le Muséon* 113 (2000), pp. 333–75. A detailed analysis of the different Patristic interpretations of Genesis 4 can be found in J.B. Glenthøj, *Cain and Abel in Syriac and Greek Writers (4th to 6th centuries)* (Corpus Scriptorum Christianorum Orientalium, Subsidia 95; Louvain, 1997).

5. Edition by E. Beck, *Des heiligen Ephraem des Syrers Hymnen de Fide* (Corpus Scriptorum Christianorum Orientalium, Scriptores Syri 73; Louvain, 1955). Translation in my *A Garland of Hymns from the Early Church* (St Athanasius' Coptic Publishing Center, 1989); vocalized text and translation in S.P. Brock and G.A. Kiraz, *Ephrem the Syrian. Select Poems* (Provo, 2006), no. 3. Another English translation of this poem, by A.N. Palmer, can be found in his "The Merchant of Nisibis: Saint Ephrem and his faithful quest for union in numbers," in J. den Boeft and A. Hilhorst (eds), *Early Christian Poetry. A Collection of Essays* (Supplement 22 to Vigiliae Christianae; Leiden, 1993), pp. 167–233, at p. 175.

6. Edition in my *Soghyatha mgabbyatha* [Select Dialogue Poems] (Monastery of St Ephrem, Holland, 1982), no. 2. Translation and commentary in my "Syriac poetry on biblical themes, 2: A dialogue poem on the sacrifice of Isaac," in *The Harp: A Review of Syriac and Oriental Studies* (Kottayam) 7 (1994), pp. 55–72.

7. Edition, translation, and commentary in my "Two Syriac verse homilies on the Binding of Isaac," in *Le Muséon* 99 (1986), pp. 61–129 (reprinted in *From Ephrem to Romanos. Interactions between Syriac and Greek in Late Antiquity* (Aldershot, 1999), Ch. VI).

8. Edition, translation, and commentary in my "Jacob of Serugh's verse homily on Tamar (Gen 38)," in *Le Muséon* 115 (2002), pp. 279–315.

9. Edition in *Soghyatha mgabbyatha,* no. 3; edition, translation and commentary in my "Joseph and Potiphar's Wife (Genesis 39): two anonymous dispute poems," in W.J. van Bekkum, J.W. Drijvers, and A.C. Klugkist (eds), *Syriac Polemics. Studies in Honour of Gerrit Jan Reinink* (Orientalia Lovaniensia Analecta 170; Leuven, 2007), pp. 41–57.

10. Edition by E. Beck, *Des heiligen Ephraem des Syrers Paschahymnen* (Corpus Scriptorum Christianorum Orientalium, Scriptores Syri 108; Louvain, 1964). Translation in my *The Harp of the Spirit: 18 Poems of St Ephrem* (Studies Supplementary to Sobornost, 2nd edn London, 1983), no. 6. Vocalized text and translation in Brock and Kiraz, *Ephrem the Syrian. Select Poems*, no.11.

11. Edition by E. Beck, *Des heiligen Ephraem des Syrers Hymnen de Fide.* Translation in *A Garland of Hymns.*

12. Edition, translation, and commentary in my "A Syriac verse homily on Elijah and the Widow of Sarepta," in *Le Muséon* 102 (1989), pp. 93–113.

IV. New Testament

1. Edition in *Soghyatha mgabbyatha,* no. 5.

2. Edition in *Soghyatha mgabbyatha,* no. 6. Translation in my *Bride of Light. Hymns on Mary from the Syriac Churches* (Piscataway NJ, 2010), no. 41.

3. Edition in *Soghyatha mgabbyatha,* no. 7. Translation in *Bride of Light,* no. 42.

4. Edition in my *Luqqate d-memre d-ʿal ktabay qudsha/Eight Syriac Mimre on Biblical Themes* (Monastery of St Ephrem, Holland, 1993), no. 7. Translation in *Bride of Light,* no. 47.

5. Edition in *Soghyatha mgabbyatha,* no. 8. (The text is also to be found as Soghitha IV in E. Beck, *Des heiligen Ephraem des Syrers Hymnen de Nativitate (Epiphania)* Corpus Scriptorum Christianorum Orientalium 82; Louvain, 1959). Translation in *Bride of Light,* no. 43.

6. Edition in *Soghyatha mgabbyatha,* no. 9 (The text is also to be found as Soghitha V in Beck, *Des heiligen Ephraem des Syrers Hymnen de Nativitate [Epiphania]).*

7. Edition by E. Beck, *Des heiligen Ephraem des Syrers Sermones II* (Corpus Scriptorum Christianorum Orientalium, Scriptores Syri 134; Louvain, 1970), and my *Luqqate.* (The translation here is based on the longer text in *Luqqate,* no. 8, where there are several differences from Beck's edition, which prints the shorter text of a different manuscript).

8. Edition, translation, and commentary in my "The Sinful Woman and Satan: two Syriac dialogue poems," in *Oriens Chris-*

tianus 72 (1988), pp. 21–62. (The text is also edited in *Soghyatha mgabbyatha,* no. 11). A translation of Jacob of Serugh's verse homily on the Sinful Woman is given by S.F. Johnson, "The Sinful Woman: a memra by Jacob of Serugh," in *Sobornost/Eastern Churches Review* 24 (2002), pp. 56–88.

9. Edition in *Soghyatha mgabbyatha,* no. 12. Translation with introduction in my The Dialogue between the Two Thieves," *The Harp* 20:1 (2006), pp. 151–70.

10. Edition in *Soghyatha mgabbyatha,* no. 13, and (with translation) in *Hugoye* 5:2 (2002), pp. 169–93. Among the several other editions, especial mention should be made of that by F.A. Pennacchietti, *Il ladrone e il cherubino. Dramma liturgico cristiano orientale in siriaco e neoaramaico* (Torino, 1993). The quotation in the Introduction is from F.F. Irving, "Easter in Ula, Salmas," in the *Archbishop's Assyrian Mission, Quarterly Paper* 21 (October 1895), pp. 118–9 (I am most grateful to Dr J.F. Coakley for supplying me with the text of this).

11. Edition by E. Beck, *Des heiligen Ephraem des Syrers Carmina Nisibena* (Corpus Scriptorum Christianorum Orientalium, Scriptores Syri 102; Louvain, 1963). Translation in *A Garland of Hymns.* Vocalized text and translation in Brock and Kiraz, *Ephrem the Syrian: Select Poems,* no. 13.

12. Edition, translation, and commentary my "Mary and the Gardener: an East Syrian dialogue *soghitha* for the Resurrection," in *Parole de l'Orient* 11 (1983), pp. 223–34.

V. From Bible to Liturgy

1. Edition in T.J. Lamy, *Sancti Ephraemi Syri Hymni et Sermones,* III (Malines, 1889), cols. 969–74. Translation in *Bride of Light,* no. 25.

2. Edition by Beck, *Des heiligen Ephraem des Syrers Hymnen de Nativitate (Epiphania).* Translation in *Bride of Light,* no. 3. A com-

plete translation of Ephrem's Hymns on the Nativity can be found in K. McVey, *Ephrem the Syrian: Hymns* (The Classics of Western Spirituality; Mahwah, NJ, 1989).

3. Edition by Beck, *Des heiligen Ephraem des Syrers Hymnen de Nativitate (Epiphania)*.

4. Edition, translation, and commentary in my "An anonymous hymn for Epiphany," in *Parole de l'Orient* 15 (1988/9), pp. 169–200.

5. Edition by E. Beck, *Des heiligen Ephraem des Syrers Hymnen de Ieiunio* (Corpus Scriptorum Christianorum Orientalium, Scriptores Syri 106; Louvain, 1964). Translation in my *The Harp of the Spirit*, no. 13. Vocalized text and translation in Brock and Kiraz, *Ephrem the Syrian: Select Poems*, no. 10.

6. Text in British Library, Add. 14614, ff.123v–126r; most of the stanzas translated are to be found in *Breviarum iuxta Ritum Ecclesiae Antiochenae Syrorum*, VI (Mosul, 1895), pp. 434–5 and 449–50; the manuscript has some further stanzas at the beginning, but these have been omitted here.

7. Edition in *Breviarium iuxta Ritum Ecclesiae Antiochenae Syrorum*, VI, pp. 140–1.

8. Introduction, edition, and translation in my "A prayer song by St Jacob of Serugh recovered," in G.A. Kiraz (ed.), *Jacob of Serugh and his Times* (Piscataway, NJ, 2010), pp. 29–37; translation in "An acrostic poem on the soul by Jacob of Serugh," in *Sobornost: Eastern Churches Review* 23 (2001), pp. 40–44.

9. Edition in Beck, *Des heiligen Ephraem des Syrers Hymnen de Nativitate (Epiphania)*, Soghitha VI.

10. Edition in E. Beck, *Des heiligen Ephraem des Syrers Hymnen de Fide*. Translation in *A Garland of Hymns*. Vocalized text and translation in Brock and Kiraz, *Ephrem the Syrian. Select Poems*, no. 17. Another English translation, by R. Murray, can be found in his "A hymn of St Ephrem to Christ on the Incarnation, the Holy Spirit and the Sacraments," in *Eastern Churches Review* 3 (1970), pp. 142–50.

11. Edition in *Teksa da-ʿmada, d-zuwwaga, d-ʿupaya* (Pampakuda, 1979), pp. 128–32.

12. Edition in *Soghyatha mgabbyatha*, no. 20. English translation in my "A dialogue between Soul and Body: an example of a long-lived Mesopotamian genre," in *Aram* 1 (1989), pp. 53–64. English translations of two of the three other Syriac dialogues between Body and Soul are available as follows: (1) by Jacob of Serugh: H.J.W. Drijvers, "Body and Soul, a perennial problem," in G.J. Reinink and H.L.J. Vanstiphout (eds), *Dispute Poems and Dialogues in the Ancient and Medieval Near East* (Orientalia Lovaniensia Analecta 42; Leuven, 1991), pp. 121–34; (2) anonymous, in the East Syriac liturgical book known as the Hudra: my "Tales of two beloved brothers: Syriac dialogues between Body and Soul," in L.S.B. MacCoull (ed.), *Studies in the Christian East in Memory of Mirrit Boutros Ghali* (Washington DC, 1995), pp. 29–38, reprinted in my *From Ephrem to Romanos*, chapter IX.

Index of Biblical References

References are to the translated texts only; these are cited by Chapter + number + stanza/line; R = Refrain

Index of Names

POPULAR PATRISTICS SERIES

ST VLADIMIR'S SEMINARY PRESS
1-800-204-2665 • www.svspress.com